Twelve Two

How to Transform Your Mind

R. LANCE PARKER, PH.D.

ISBN 979-8-88540-829-5 (paperback)
ISBN 979-8-89043-646-7 (hardcover)
ISBN 979-8-88540-830-1 (digital)

Christian Faith Publishing
832 Park Avenue
Meadville, PA 16335
www.christianfaithpublishing.com

Printed in the United States of America

I would like to thank Pastor Mike Snow of Gracepoint
Church in Wichita, Kansas, for his countless
hours of wise counsel and inspiration.

For my wife, Tish, who has been so patient, supportive,
and encouraging throughout the writing of this book.
Thank you for walking this journey with me.

For my son, Ryan, who has shown me how to be still and enjoy
every single moment of life. Ryan, you are the best son ever!

Contents

Introduction

Sometimes when I conduct seminars, teaching people how to change their thinking, I will open "the show" with something unexpected. For example, once when I spoke at a church, the pastor began the first night of the seminar by giving me a nice, traditional introduction. As the crowd politely applauded, I entered the building, riding a motorcycle while the song "If You Want Blood You've Got It" by AC/DC blared on the sound system. My intention was to shock everyone into challenging their beliefs and expectations of what a seminar by a psychologist, sponsored by a church, *should* be. Mission accomplished. People sat with mouths wide open, clapping, and elbowing each other.

I then explained to the audience, "So, motorcycles in the church, AC/DC, rock and roll in the church, scandalous! But that is the point. That is why we are here tonight—a crash course in transforming how you think. Something I learned from Pastor Mike Snow—it is okay to reclaim my music. Growing up, I listened to rock and roll. I listened to all those bad boy songs, and when I got saved, suddenly I felt like I couldn't listen to the music anymore. If it came on the radio, I felt kind of guilty for tapping my foot or singing along. But Pastor Snow taught me to make the music my own. One day, I was driving around, and this song [If You Want Blood You've Got It by AC/DC] came on the radio, and for the first time, I heard it differently. I literally saw it differently. As the song played, I imagined Jesus and the twelve disciples speaking to me." I walked through each line of the song with the audience and had them listen to the lyrics as if Jesus was speaking each line directly to them. This is a very powerful exercise that anyone can do to begin learning how to change their perspective of a situation.

Now obviously, this stunt is less impactful simply reading it in a book. The exercise is designed to get the audience to begin to see that they can control their thinking and can shift their perspective of life to create a new experience. So if you are reading this and you are not familiar with this song, I strongly recommend you set the book down for a minute, pull the song up, and listen to it. See Jesus's face. See him speaking to you. Try to hear the lyrics coming from him rather than the band. Endeavor to shift your perspective, and perceive a new meaning from the song—a meaning of love and sacrifice.

This book was designed to teach you a basic truth. You and only you control what you think. I learned this truth in my studies to become a psychologist. But consider what Paul said: "transform by the renewing of your mind." He was saying, "Learn to think differently." So obviously, you control what you think, or Paul would not have told you to change how you think—renew your mind. So why did Paul implore us to change how we think? Finish the verse: "…so you will be able to discern and test the good and perfect will of God." And isn't that what we all want? Don't you want to know why you are here? What is the purpose of it all? What is the meaning of life?

As a psychologist, I have studied, developed, and practiced the art of cognitive behavioral therapy (CBT). Cognitive refers to thought, think, perception. Behavioral refers to behaviors, actions, speech. By changing how we think and behave, we can change how we feel, our experiences. I have strived to help my patients and clients learn to think differently so they may alleviate their anxiety, depression, guilt, and anger so they may free themselves from addictions or improve relationships at work or at home. Essentially, I have helped people "transform by the renewing of their mind." It took me a few years to realize, these cognitive restructuring skills are actually not new at all. The Bible is filled with them, and I would daresay, a majority of the New Testament is aimed specifically at teaching us to change how we think so that we may enjoy a closer relationship with God, learn his will for our lives, and receive the blessings he is pouring out.

The goal of this book is twofold: first the goal is to explain "cognitive restructuring" in a language the reader can understand

and provide specific steps to follow to begin using these skills immediately in their personal life. The second goal is to show the reader that with these simple yet powerful skills, you can actually begin to develop a deeper and more meaningful relationship with God.

Cognitive Restructuring

Perspective—what you *see* is what *you* see. When you looked at the photo below, many of you, when you first glanced at it, saw a man looking right at you. But some of you saw a man looking to the right. And now that I mention the other perspective, you are now able to shift back and forth in your mind and see a man looking right at you or see a man looking to the right. In this book, that is what I am hoping to help you learn how to do with your mental perspective of all matters—control how you think so you can intentionally shift between perspectives to create the experience you want.

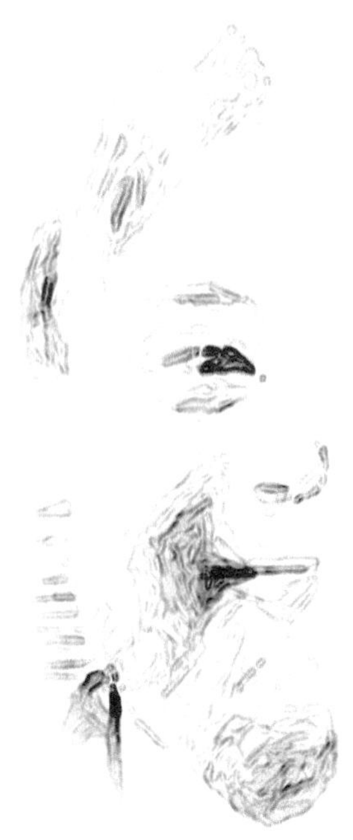

Cognitive restructuring (or reframing) simply refers to changing how you think, not just *what* you think about but *how* you think about something.

For example, you could choose to think *about* the glass of water or choose to think *about* something else. This is an example of changing *what* you think about. Many of us use this as a coping mechanism. We will try to not think *about* something that upsets us. We will choose to think *about* other things and distract ourselves—television, movies, social media, projects, friends, etc. This is effective to a degree.

But what you don't realize is that you have the power to change *how* you think about something. We have all heard the philosophical question: "Is the glass half empty or half full?" That represents *how* you think about something—your *perspective*. What you are really asking is, "Do you think negatively or positively?" Most people assume that is just who they are, and there is nothing they can do about it. But that is not true. You can *change your perspective* through cognitive restructuring.

Introduction to the Four
Fundamentals

The idea that there are four basic fundamental thought processes that underlie all thinking was born out of what I do for a living. I am a psychologist, and I have been practicing for over twenty years. I have worked in jails, prisons, hospitals, drug rehabs, corporations, and in private practice. A majority of my practice for years centered around high-conflict couples and families engaged in divorce and child custody battles.

During this time, I began to notice that all issues—whether personal, professional, or relationship—had common underpinnings. As I studied my clients more and more, I found that I could trace the root of most problems, issues, conflicts, etc. to four specific *fundamental* cognitive distortions (distorted beliefs or thought processes). This helped me really focus quickly on the true source of problems people were experiencing.

As I testified in court to the source of parental conflicts and how best to resolve matters, judges began to approach me outside of court, asking me to teach these fundamental skills to all parents going through a divorce. You see, the judges made this request because they know how conflictual and how troubling divorces and child custody disputes can be for those parents, and they wanted the parents to be able to have this information so they would be able to cope better with the tragedy of divorce and to have better coparenting relationships.

So this information, these Four Fundamental cognitive-restructuring skills were born out of my study of psychology and validated as valuable by courts. Now I did not invent them myself. Great psychologists, psychiatrists, and academicians in years past worked to develop the constructs and identify common irrational beliefs and cognitive distortions. All I did was zone in on the four most common of these and try to package them into something people could actually understand and find useful. (This is an important point that I will come back to.)

I also taught anger-management classes for years. One year, I offered to serve the church by teaching the class in the building and letting the church charge a fee. When I first did this, Pastor Mike Snow sat through the first series of classes. For me, this was a little unnerving because every time I would look over at him, he had a solid blank stare on his face, and I couldn't get a read on how he was responding to the course material. I finally worked up the courage and asked him, "Are you okay with what I am teaching in your church?" Pastor Snow squinted at me for a minute then slowly and quietly replied, "There's a lot of good stuff here." This led to many conversations with the pastor over the next few months. We talked about the class material, the Bible, Jesus, and we both began to see how these fundamental cognitive-restructuring skills were not just useful to managing anger, anxiety, depression, improving careers, and improving relationships; these are what the Fundamentals were originally for, and this was how I used the information every day in my private practice to help people suffering from all sorts of maladies. But in my talks with the pastor, I began to have my eyes opened to how these fundamental skills could be applied to our spiritual walk. For example, if we are not feeling connected with our partner or if we are not feeling connected with ourselves, do we have the tools to *feel connected to Jesus?*

And so, over time, out of these pastoral discussions, the Four Fundamentals were born. They form the core and the building blocks of improving all areas of your emotional experiences and your life. And they are the building blocks for you to start having a deeper, more meaningful relationship with Jesus and with the Bible. Rather than seeing the Bible as a list of rules—"this is all the stuff I can't do"—the Four Fundamentals help you to start looking at the Bible as an instruction guide written just for you to help you have a good, joy-filled, and meaningful life. If you have ever asked, "I want to know what God's plan is for me," well the answer is written in the Bible somewhere. But it is up to you to dig into it and start pulling it out. The Bible was written for you. It wasn't written for them. So if you are reading the Bible and you are thinking about other people, you are disconnecting from the Bible and from Jesus. But if you will look into the Bible to get information for *yourself,* then your eyes will start to be opened.

One of the first times that happened for me, Pastor Snow and I were in a men's Bible study on a Wednesday morning at 6:30 a.m. I just happened to open my Bible to Matthew 15:16, and I started giggling to myself. Everyone in the group said, "What?" I said, "Right here, Jesus says to his disciples, 'What? Are you being willfully stupid?'" Everyone began turning to that scripture, and we all got a chuckle out of the fact that something like that was actually in the Bible. Then Pastor Snow leaned over, looked me in the eye, and said, "You know, that was written for you and me." Touché. And he was right. What was happening in that passage right before then, Jesus had been approached by the Pharisees with one of these conundrums in which they were trying to trap him, and Jesus's response was just brilliant. I could just see Jesus giving this answer then dropping the microphone. I could see the Pharisees standing there, mouths agape, saying, "Rats! He got us!" Then as Jesus walked off, his followers ran up to him and said, "What were you talking about? What was that about? I don't get it." And Jesus explained it again, but they still didn't get it. Then Jesus looked at them and said, "What? Are you willfully being stupid?" Notice, implied in the question is that we have a choice: to be stupid or not, to understand or not. These are *thought processes,* and again, we see that we have been given the control over how we think and thus the ability to change how we think. Jesus often used metaphors and allegories when he spoke. He did this on purpose to challenge us to inspect how we think about things and then change how we think.

As we go through the Four Fundamentals in this book, here is how I want you to think of them. I once heard an interview with

Tom Brady. He's unquestionably the world's greatest quarterback. The interviewer noted that he had seen Tom practicing before every game. He asked Tom, "What's that little yellow scrap of paper on your clipboard you have out there?" Tom smiled bashfully and hung his head. He then said, "Back in college, a quarterback coach came to me and watched me throw the football. He then scribbled on this paper and said, 'These are the Four Fundamentals to a forward pass. I want you to practice them every day for thirty minutes.'" So the world's greatest quarterback, making millions a year on the eve of the Super Bowl—what is he practicing? Reading the defense? Trick plays? No. This is what he practices:

1. Make a chicken wing.
2. Grip the laces.
3. Come over the top.
4. Flick the wrist.

And because he focuses so much on getting the fundamentals down, he can handle the advanced elements of the game more easily. As I heard this, I began thinking, maybe life is like that. Maybe there are just a few fundamentals; and if we can get those fundamentals down, then maybe we can handle the advanced elements of life more easily.

Perspective

One way to understand perspective (perception, frame of mind, belief system) is to consider sunglasses. Perceptions are like sunglasses. If you look up at the lights in the ceiling right now, you will see a white light radiating from the light fixture. Now if I gave you a pair of sunglasses that had a yellow tinting and you put them on then looked at the light again, the light would now appear yellow. So let's establish what just happened. When you view the light through clear lenses or no lenses, it appears white. When you view the light through tinted lenses, the light appears yellow.

Now, a very important question: In the scenario above, *what* changed that *caused* your mental experience of the light to change from white to yellow? Did *reality* change (light bulb)? No. But your *mental experience* changed. What *caused* the change in your experience was whether you chose to look at the light through the sunglasses or not. Sunglasses are *filters*. Depending on the *filter* you choose, your experience of the reality around you changes. And notice, *you* choose the sunglasses you want based on the visual *experience* you want to have. You will stand in the store for thirty minutes trying on different sunglasses then look around the store to determine if that particular pair brings you the visual *experience you want* or not.

Understand that we have *mental filters* that we load into our brain that act much like sunglasses. You can't see them like you can sunglasses, but they are there just the same. These *mental filters* are called *perceptions or perspectives*. You already know this, you just didn't know you know. Consider how many times have you disagreed with someone about something, and you said to them, "Well that ain't how *I see it*." Now you are not referring to your actual vision and eyeballs. You are referring to your mental *perspective* on a matter. There is one reality, but you and the other person are having two different experiences. Maybe they're upset, but you're happy. Or you're upset, and they're happy. But it is the same reality for both of you. When you say, "That is not how I see it," you are declaring that how you mentally *perceive* the matter is determining your *experience*.

This is really important to understand in cognitive behavioral psychology. Cognitive behavioral theory operates on the model that you and I are comprised of three basic components: thoughts, behaviors, and feelings. A lot of times, people come to the psychologist because they want to change how they feel. But we can't just change our feelings. Go ahead and try: "feel happy!" Didn't work, did it? You can't turn your *experience* on and off like a light switch, but you can change how you *think* and what you *do*.

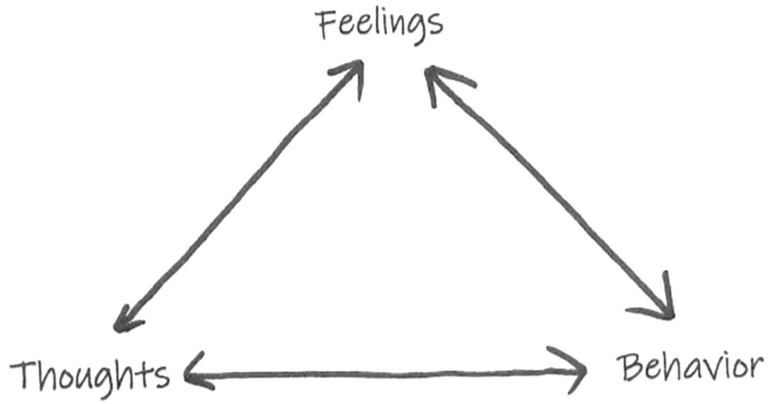

So consider this example: If I wake up in the morning and *I feel* "bleh" I may then *think, Oh, to heck with it. I'm not going to work today. Screw it.* Now I will probably *behave* by rolling over and going back to sleep. Two hours later, when I wake up again and look at the clock, I may *think, You really screwed the pooch now. You're so stupid. You went back to sleep instead of getting up for work. You're so lazy.* I am judging myself harshly (*thoughts about self*). How am I going to *feel* about myself based on these judgmental *thoughts?* Negatively *judging* myself will generate more negative *feelings.* So as I *think* negative *thoughts* about myself, I begin to *feel* even worse than when I woke up that morning. Now that I am *feeling* worse and I am *thinking* I am such a loser, what *behaviors* do you think are coming to my mind as I lie in bed? Stay in bed. Roll over. Go back to sleep. What about the *behavior* of going to work? That is probably way down the list of options and may seem impossible to do at this point.

Notice how I *think* leads to what I *feel* and generates options of how to *act.* How I *feel* influences how I *think* and how I *act.* How I *act* contributes to how I *feel* and think about *myself.* Thus, if I *think* a certain way and *behave* a certain way, I am going to create certain *feelings.* And in the example above, clearly, the thoughts and behaviors were the driver of depressive feelings.

This is how thinking fits into our experiences in life and why I want to target *thinking* in this book the most because all your life you have been trying to change your *behavior,* and you keep ending up back in the exact same situation or circumstance. You may make a New Year's resolution: "Hey, I am going to do this!" or you promise someone you will stop doing something and you start forcing yourself to behave differently, but you never seem to maintain the new behavior for very long. Maybe you want a deeper relationship with Jesus, so you force yourself to go to church or you force yourself to read the Bible. But as you may have noticed, just forcing a change in behavior is never enough. You don't feel it, and you don't feel connected to Jesus. You don't understand what the Bible is really saying, so it is not long before you have regressed back to the old behaviors and old patterns.

There's another purpose to learning to think differently. Certainly, you can improve your mood, reduce anxiety, and manage your anger and addiction better. But I believe the whole point of the New Testament is to begin to think differently. I am not trying to oversell this, so let me warn you now, just reading this book will not bring about any change. When you finish the last page, you will not suddenly be a new person. And if you take my advice and begin working on restructuring your cognitions (changing how you think), you probably won't see much of a change in the first week or two. That is not realistic and is not the goal of all of this. Think about working out. How complicated is it? It is *fundamentally* really simple. You pick up a heavy object, then you lower it back down. That's it! But just doing it once does not produce any results. To see results from your work, you must perform the simple exercise thirty times a day for a couple of weeks. *Then* you can look in the mirror and begin to see the *growth*, the *progress*. It is the same thing with the cognitive-restructuring *exercises* you are about to learn. They will sound very simple, and you may even say, "Oh yeah, I get it." But that is not enough. If you perform these simple mental exercises thirty times a day, consistently, for weeks, *then* you can look in the mirror and begin to see the personal *growth*, the *progress*.

Paul said in Romans 12:2, "Transform yourself by the renewing of your mind…" Change how you think. Renew your mind. Begin to think differently, and you will begin to transform yourself. Notice, he chose the word "transform." He did not say, "Instantly become."

Transformation takes time. How much time it takes is entirely up to you. How often will you work on understanding the Four Fundamentals? How many times in a week or a day or an hour will you actively monitor your thought life and reframe your thoughts? Even Paul wrote that he had not yet achieved all that he was instructing us to do. But he said he pressed on striving to obtain the goal.

What are those goals? There are many, and they are entirely up to you. For example, do you want to be able to discern God's will for your life? Have peace? Experience a deeper relationship with Jesus? Stop worrying and start trusting? Whatever your goal is, get busy transforming by reading the next chapter.

Fundamental Number One

In my time working with people from a cognitive-behavioral per-spective, I have found the most effective way to teach someone that Fundamental #1 is through an illustration. I could just tell it to them. I have tried this, and they always agree. That is because they already know it. And you already know what I am about to tell you too, but you just don't *understand* what it truly means. And in reality, you don't actually believe it. Whether it is crowd of two hundred or a single client, invariably I invite others to participate in a role play with me. So as the reader, I am asking you to join in and participate with me in the following role play:

> Imagine that you have entered my office for the first time and are seated on the couch. You're sitting there, and maybe it is the first time you have ever met a psychologist. And there I am, a doctor. But I am extremely anxious, and I keep shooting nervous glances at the window. It is clear to you that I am distracted by something outside. But I tighten my grip on the arm of my chair, grit my teeth and force myself to smile and speak to you. "Welcome! Uhm…what was your name?" But before you can answer, I glance to the window again and nervously shift in my chair. I turn back to you and stare blankly for a minute, as if I forgot what I was doing.

This goes on for a few minutes, and I finally explain in an anx-ious voice, "I am so sorry! But I left my car window down out in the parking lot, and it kinda looks like it is about to rain. Oh goodness! I don't know what to do. You know what? That isn't your problem. I will shut up about the rain. Okay. Where was I at?" I try very hard to shift my focus back to you, and I begin to talk again when, suddenly, I shift my attention back to the window. "Was that thunder?" I then turn back to you and say, "Don't you hate it when your car seats get wet, and you have to sit in them and ride home? And then, the next day, they smell like mildew and…Oh goodness! There I go again! I am really sorry about this. Okay. I will let it go. I'll just forget about the rain. Now, what were we talking about?"

Now imagine I keep this up for fifteen minutes. I remain anxious and keep glancing out the window. I try to focus on you, but my worry about the rain getting my car seats wet continually wins out. Eventually, you would tell me to go do what? (This is your part in the role play. State your answer out loud right now.)

Every time I do this role play, it doesn't matter if it is an individual session or a large crowd. It doesn't matter if the crowd volunteered to attend my seminar or if they were compelled by the court to attend. Everyone always answers the exact same way. In a voice tinged with incredulousness, like I am stupid for even asking the question, they all say, "Go roll up your car window!" And you probably said the exact same thing.

Now this is a *really important question*. So take some time to consider it before answering. You told me to go roll up my car window. Why didn't you tell me to go stop the rain? (Long pause here to let you think. Again, state your answer out loud.) And again, everyone answers the question the exact same way, "You can't control the rain."

That is a fact. You cannot control the weather. It is a *truth*. And more importantly, you *believe it* (thought process). Now, because you *believe* you can't control the weather, notice: *It does not cross your mind!* "Is it raining? Let me go roll up the car window." Once you *understand* (thought process) the difference between the things you can't control and the things you can control, and once you *believe* it, notice how quickly you *shift your attention* (thought process) away from the thing you don't control over to the things you do control.

Fundamental #1. *There are five things in this world you cannot control any more than the rain.*

1. *The past.* You can't change what has already been done. Enough said.

2. *The future.* It hasn't happened yet. How do you undo something that hasn't occurred? How do you control something that hasn't even taken place? How do change something you can't even *predict?* You cannot even predict the future. Look at the stock market and all these people getting paid lots of money to predict the stock market. You would think somebody would actually be able to do it. Research I just read recently said that 97 percent of all stock analysts do worse than the average. And these are the professionals trained to predict stock trends and futures! You cannot predict the future. When you were eighteen years old, did you think this is where your life would end up?

3. *You cannot control what other people think.* How many arguments have you had trying to change someone's mind? Through gritted teeth, you barked, "If you would just understand!" Look at politics. People literally spend billions of dollars every year trying to control how the public *thinks* about their candidate or trying to change public *opinion.* Has it ever worked on you?

4. *You cannot control what another person does.* Am I telling you anything new? You can't control other people's behavior. Impossible. Would the jails be filled if we could control behavior? Don't you think that, as a society, we'd eliminate one or two crimes if we could actually control how people acted?

5. *And you cannot control what another person feels.* How many sad love songs have been written because "she's lost that loving feeling"? Think about it. There would be no break-ups or divorces. If we could control people's feelings, don't you think that, as a psychologist, I would have cashed in

on it a long time ago? People come to therapy all the time, wanting to feel happier. If I actually had the ability to cause someone to no longer feel depressed and to start feeling happy, don't you think I would?

To recap so far, Fundamental #1 is a *truth*. You cannot control the past, the future, what other people think, what other people do, and what other people feel. Most people will nod their head in agreement. At some level, you already know this. Why am I harping on it if I know you already know? There is a difference between knowledge and wisdom. You may know something, but if you don't apply it or really *believe* it, you can't benefit from the knowledge.

Now for the hard part. Once you accept that you cannot (at all) control the past, the future, what others think, what others do, and you can't control what someone else feels, then answer this question: What do you control?

At this point, you are probably saying, "Myself." A lot of people answer that way. But that is a vague answer, and vagaries do not lead to solutions. To illustrate, let's say you invited me to dinner and spent the whole day cooking. I arrive and eat. After dinner, you look over and say, "So? What did you think of the meal?" And I reply, "Meah." You think, *Meah? What the heck is meah? What does that even mean?* Notice, no specifics are coming to your mind. But imagine if instead I replied, "Well the biscuits were a little doughy, and the chili was kind of bland." Now notice what is happening to you mentally. You are thinking about leaving the biscuits in the oven longer and adding more spices to the chili. When your brain is given specifics, your mind can generate specific solutions, answers, or responses.

So specifically, Fundamental #1 says there are four things *you do control* (just think the opposite of what you don't control):

1. *You can control the present.* Not a second before or after, just right now.
2. *You can control what and how you think.* Inside this very moment, you control your thought life.

3. *You can control what you do.* Options come to your mind how to behave, and you are the only one who can choose to act.
4. *You can control what you feel.*

Think about that last one for a moment. You control how you feel. Yes, you do. Remember, you just agreed, "I cannot control what another person feels." Well *they are saying the same thing about you,* "It ain't my fault they feel that way! Nuh-uh." So if you can't control how they feel, then they can't control how you feel. So who controls how you feel? You do. So, yes, I am saying, if you are depressed, if you are angry, frustrated, anxious, despondent, if you are whatever, *it is your own fault.*

That is a rude way of putting it, but I do so to help create a memory. If someone asks you, "How was that book?" Turn to them and say, "Dr. Parker said it's all my fault!" I am trying to shake up your brain and get you to stop imprisoning yourself.

I am bringing something to you completely different than what you have heard from others. *It is your fault* if you are depressed, angry, frustrated. *And this is the best news you will ever get from any-one.* Nobody and nothing controls you! Think about it. You agreed; I can't control what someone else feels, so they can't control what you feel. Carry it on out. Whatever you are feeling, you must be creating. So this means if you can create depression, *you can create happiness.* If you can create anxiety, *you can create serenity.* If you can create anger, *you can create peace.* If you can create frustration, *you can create patience.*

You trap yourself when you choose to view the world through negative perspectives. If I can get you to step back and look around at your world differently, *you could free yourself.*

Every single experience in your entire life is 100 percent under your control right here, right now. You have the power to experience whatever you want. And what dumbfounds me about this is, in all the years that I have practiced psychology, I haven't heard a lot of that in literature. I see these tools they have given us to help people. But what I hear researchers and clinicians talk about is, you can't cure depression. You can't cure anxiety. You can only manage it. That is such a hopeless message: "You are depressed because of how you think. Only you can change how you think. But we don't think you will ever not be depressed. You just need to get used to the idea of being depressed your whole life and start trying to manage it."

Truth: You can't control the past, future, what others think, do, or feel. Trying to control these things is like trying to stop the rain from falling. You do control the present, what you think, do, and feel. This is like rolling up the car window. Are you seeing the power yet? Because you *believe* you can't control the rain, your mind instantly turns to the thing you do control: the car window. The same can happen for your life the sooner you come to fully believe

Fundamental #1: I can't control the past, so let me live in the present. I can't control what others think, so let me focus on what I think. I can't control what others do, so let me focus on how I want to feel in this situation.

Get this, *the Bible already told us all of this!* In Proverbs, it says, "A person without self-control is like a city being broken into and left without walls." Think about that for a second. If *you* don't control *yourself, you* make *yourself* completely vulnerable to attacks from outside of you. Why are you vulnerable? Why are you suffering? Why are you depressed? Why are you anxious? I know I said it's your fault, but you don't know what you don't know. When we violate Fundamental #1, we *give away control* of ourselves to the past, the future, and to other people. We make ourselves vulnerable to attacks from the outside. And this is even more important in this time of social media. Facebook, Twitter, and all the others are constantly pumping negative information at you. And even worse than that are the trolls that sit around in their underwear in their mother's basement, indignantly sniping and attacking you through their random, unsolicited negative comments. It has led people to depression, anxiety, and worse yet, this whole concept of canceling a person out. But it is not their fault; it is *yours.* When *you* develop self-control, *you* are no longer vulnerable to the attacks from the world.

Remember this *truth*: Only you have control over what you think, do, and *feel.* And the only time you have control over is *right now.* So begin developing *self-control,* for it is the pathway to freedom and peace. In doing so, you will be following God's will for your life. Think about it, Jesus asked his disciples, "Why are you trying to get that speck of dust out of your brother's eye when you got a plank in your own eye? Why don't your first get the plank out of your eye, then you can see better to go after that speck of dust."

When I am working with someone, I spend a lot of time helping them understand Fundamental #1. So when they come to session and they are struggling and upset with something someone said or did, I will simply ask, "What is Fundamental #1?" Oftentimes, they will sigh, hang their head, and say, "I know I can't control what they do." But this is not the point of Fundamental #1. Why is it so important for you to recognize the things you cannot control? *So you can quickly get your attention onto the things you do control!* You are not a victim. You are no one's fool. You are powerful. Learn to harness your God-given power.

Notice, you point this filter, Fundamental #1, at yourself as well. You see yourself through this lens. If you are focusing on your past, you will begin experiencing depression, regret, guilt, or shame. Maybe you feel depressed because your marriage fell apart, or your life didn't go the way you wanted it to, or something happened to you when you were twelve years old. The past is over. You can't change it. But by living in it, you keep the past alive every single day. You give power to the past and cause yourself to continually experience the same emotions over and over.

Or you point Fundamental #1 at your future. This will cause you to start experiencing worry, anxiety, fear, trepidation, and doubt. If you are not focused on this present moment, but instead you are living in that future that you are worrying about, you will create the distress today that you are hoping to avoid tomorrow. The problem is, *it is always today, so you will always be creating stress.*

And we point this filter at other people. If you are focused on what others think, you begin creating drama. Can you read minds? No. But you will act like you can. You assume they think something and then act on your assumption: "Oh, they said that because they think (fill in the blank). And since they think that, well I am going to do this!" You just end up creating the very drama you complain about.

If you are focused on what other people are doing, then you are going to come across as angry, critical, and demanding or controlling because you will be led to criticize them or tell them what they are doing wrong. Or you will feel like what other people are doing is victimizing you. So you make your experience the result of their behavior. You turn yourself into a victim and make yourself dependent on others. You feel helpless, powerless. This leads to conflict because if their behavior causes you to feel bad, then the only way for you to feel good is for them to change. You don't want to be a victim, but you feel like one, so you may lash out at them and try to make them stop doing something or start doing something.

If you are focusing on what other people feel, you might be seen as controlling or manipulative. Because if they should feel a certain way, you incorrectly believe you have to do something to cause them to feel that way. "What can I do to make them happy?" Or you may feel helpless because nothing you do makes them feel what you want.

I learned this in graduate school in the nineties. This was part of the course curriculum to become a psychologist. Professors taught us that we don't have the power to change how a client or patient feels. I was shocked. "Why am I here then?" I didn't get it. It took me many years to figure out that I can't control my clients. And when I finally got it, I felt liberated. Understanding and believing that I can't actually control my clients freed me to finally be able to truly help them.

This concept, this truth, Fundamental #1, was actually written down long before there were psychologists, long before universities conducted research into effective treatments for depression and anxiety, long before I attended graduate school to learn cognitive-restructuring skills. Just one example: Jesus said, "Why try to get the speck of dust out of your brother's eye when you have a big ol' log in yours? Why don't you get the plank out of your eye, then you can see better to go after that little speck in your brother's eye." What is he saying to us? *To you?* "Uh, don't be digging around in your friend's eyeball?" No. Again, he is speaking metaphorically. It is not about the eyeball. Jesus is saying, "Focus on yourself." This is what you have power over, so focus all your energy on becoming a better you.

Homework

Take some time to consider the truth of Fundamental #1. It is often easiest to see things in others before we see it in ourselves. Pay attention throughout the day, and notice how so many people are *reacting* emotionally and behaviorally to the past, future, and others. Try to look inside yourself and identify how many of your experiences are seemingly controlled by your past, your imagined future, or what others are doing or saying.

Application

Since you control yourself in the present, choose how to start each day to set the course for the type of day you would like to experience. First thing every morning, the instant you turn off your alarm, turn on something to listen to that will build you up. Inspire yourself. Take control of your thought life. Rather than letting your thoughts randomly float up (dread over getting up, worry what the day will bring, regrets over last night, etc.), choose what those first words of the day will be. Listen to a ten-minute daily devotional while you are getting your coffee and breakfast. *Above Inspiration* has some fantastic ten-minute video clips. Pull up a sermon from the Internet to listen to while you shower and fix your hair. Creflo Dollar, Joyce Meyer, Steve Furtick, or Michael Todd are all great choices. Explore and find one you like. Choose a motivational speaker to listen to. Play music that puts you in the emotional and cognitive state of mind you would like to experience. Every day is a new day. So take control of how you will experience that day by controlling what you feed your mind first thing in the morning.

Fundamental Number Two

By now, hopefully you understand that only you control yourself. Only you create your experiences. And while this may make sense academically and theoretically, it probably doesn't make sense practically. "Okay. I understand the logic of Fundamental #1. But it really felt like my wife made me mad last night!"

What leads us to violate Fundamental #1 is Fundamental #2. But violating Fundamental #2 causes so many more problems than just a violation of Fundamental #1. Here's how Fundamental #2 works:

> Think about the sunglass's analogy again. When I look at the world through yellow tinted lens, I have a mental experience of everything being yellow. But if I put on a different-colored lens, then suddenly, my mental experience of the world changes. Notice, the world is not changing, but my mental experience is *because of the filter I chose to view the world through.*

There is a very powerful *mental* filter we frequently choose to view our world through. It is called "Should Statements." This filter is known as a cognitive distortion because it actually doesn't just filter our reality, it distorts it. It is called Should Statements because, typically, that is what we say: "They should…" "She should…" "I should've…" "they shouldn't…" When we say or think the word "*should,*" it is a clue that we have chosen to view our world through this lens, this filter. The word itself is not bad. It is just a common clue to the presence of this thought process. There are other less common words we use. Words such as *must, have to, need to, gotta, supposed to expect.* We use them interchangeably, and we each may have our favorite. But regardless of which word you use, it is still a clue that you have chosen to *perceive* your world, this situation, these circumstances, through a mental filter that serves only to distort reality. Adopting this perspective of the world creates three distinct but intertwined problems for us.

Problem #1

Once we load this filter in, we create for ourselves the opportunity to only have one out of two experiences: failure or nothing, anger or nothing, frustration or nothing. We can only have a negative emotional experience after a Should Statement. Think about it, when other people are not doing what they are *supposed* to do, you get angry. If they do something they *shouldn't*, you get mad. Truth.

So how do you feel when other people are doing what they *should*? Handling things the way they *need* to be handled? At this point, you may be tempted to say "happy." But that is not true at all. It is the myth you tell yourself. Truth. When other people do what they *should*, you won't even notice it 99 percent of the time.

Perfect example: You are driving down the road, and you hit a pothole. You then think, *Man! The city should fix that!* Notice, you just said *should*, which means you are viewing the situation through a mental filter, a perceptual process, a cognitive distortion of *Should Statements.* You chose these sunglasses. The city *should* maintain the roads. They are not doing what they *should.* Thus, you have no choice but to feel angry and frustrated. Thinking it is the city's fault; and feeling angry, you begin to feel a compulsion to act on your frustration. "Grr! I am going to write a letter!" Makes perfect sense, doesn't it?

Now, think about this: When was the last time you drove an entire city block, did not hit a single pothole, and you got out of your car and thought, *Man! That is a damn fine stretch of road right there! Will you look at that! Smooth! No potholes anywhere! I think I am going to write a letter!—never!* You drive thousands of miles every year and never notice when the city is maintaining the roads as they *should*. But you hit *one* pothole, and you are fired up!

For most people, perhaps even for you, so much of your life is governed by this filter. What people *should* be doing, how they *should* be acting, what they *should* be saying, what they *should* be thinking, and you don't even recognize you are doing this to yourself all day long. Consider if you came to my office, or any office. You arrive; the doors are open. The carpet is clean. Chairs are available in the waiting room. The electricity is flowing, and the lights are on. Does that make you happy? No. You *didn't even notice* that someone vacuumed the carpet that morning and adjusted the loose doorknob. It did not register that someone chose and arranged the furniture in the waiting area, and it never crosses your mind that someone is paying the electric bill each and every month. But when these things are *not* done as they *should* be, you get upset. When they are done, you don't even notice it.

And check it out; now that I have brought it to your awareness, you still are not happy! You did not feel a sudden surge or happiness that Dr. Parker pays his electric bill. So the truth is, after a *Should Statement*, you cannot be happy. Even when you are aware that someone is doing the things you think they *should* be doing, you can't be happy or pleased or at peace. You can only have a negative experience (anger, frustration, disgust, etc.) or nothing. The best you can hope for is just not mad.

And equally troubling is, you view yourself through this filter. Think about all the times you have said or thought, "Oh, man, I *shouldn't* have said that," or "Why did I do that? I *shouldn't* have." You beat yourself up when you think or say, "I *shouldn't* have acted that way. I feel so horrible!" or "I *should've* known better. I am so stupid!" Challenge yourself right now. Honestly, try and think of a time you actually felt joy after doing something that you were *supposed* to do or *needed* to do? You drive with your hands at ten and two. Did that make you happy? You observed the speed limit. Did that make you happy? You stopped at the red light. Did your chest swell with pride? You put on clothes this morning. Did you look in the mirror and tell yourself how good it feels to pick out your own clothes? You didn't throat punch the checkout clerk who moved too slowly ringing up your groceries. Did you celebrate that decision and buy yourself an ice cream cone on the way home? When you do what you are *supposed* to do, even when you are aware you are doing it, it doesn't make you feel good. It is impossible.

Where is happiness? where is joy? where is appreciation? *It does not exist after a Should Statement.* This mental filter is not designed to generate positive experiences for you. It is only designed to distinguish between right and wrong—what should be and what should not be. The world is coming at you and passing through this filter that *you chose* to load in when you said, "They *should...*" "*I should...*" "*She should...*" "*He shouldn't...*" "*I need to...*" "*They are supposed to...*" (fill in the blank).

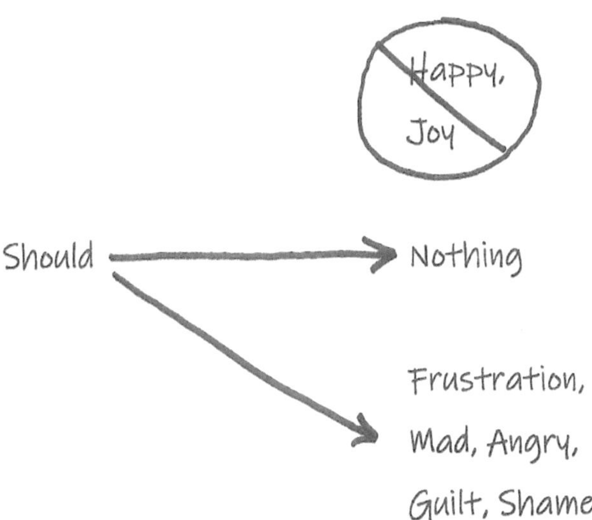

Now think about your walk with Jesus. How many times have you felt guilty for not reading the Bible? You tell yourself things like, "I should read my Bible more." Did you look forward to reading? Were you excited to start reading? Did you rush home from work and jump in bed with the book and read all night? No. You probably felt guilty because you thought you *should* be reading the Bible. Then when you told yourself you *should* start reading the Bible, you began to feel a lot of pressure and conviction to get started. You may call this pressure stress. Once you started, you did not feel happy. Instead, what you felt was *relief.* Relief is the absence of pressure. It is the absence of something bad, not the presence of something good.

Do you feel connected to God when you walk into church? Or are you thinking, *I have to be here. My wife told me I had to come.* Do you ever cry out, "What do I do? I don't feel good. I don't feel like I belong. I don't feel like Jesus is listening to me. Well maybe I *should* go to church more. Maybe I *should* go help the homeless. Maybe I *should…*" After a *Should Statement,* you cannot feel happy. You can't feel more connected. You can't feel loved. It is not in the equation. That mental filter prevents anything else from happening other than frustration, pressure, stress, guilt, or nothing.

Now, as I alluded to earlier, there is something that you mistake for happiness. It is called relief. If I were to squeeze your arm for five minutes, you would begin to feel pressure. And when I let go, you might say, "Oh, thank you so much! I feel so much better!" What just happened? You went from a neutral experience (no touch) to an experience of pressure then back to a neutral experience. And you are saying thank you?

You don't even know you are doing this exact same thing all day long. You start to get mad because someone appears to be running late, and they *should* be on time. You start to experience anticipatory frustration. But they arrive right on time, and you feel a relief from the frustration *you were creating* when you thought they *should* arrive on time, and they *should not* be late.

Or, as you drive, a car passes you. You might start thinking, *They better not cut in front of me!* Traffic becomes stressful. Then when they don't cut in front of you, the pressure dissipates, and you think you are enjoying your drive. Notice, you continually take yourself from a neutral experience (state of nothingness) to anticipatory frustration or a state of being stressed out, then back to a neutral experience (state of nothingness) when they do what they *should.*

And of course, you do this to yourself all day long. You are sitting there, experiencing nothing when you suddenly remember you *gotta* get the laundry done. Pressure and stress instantly begin building. Or you tell yourself, "I *need* to get all this work done before 5:00 p.m." and suddenly feel stressed. You create the stress and pressure for yourself. Then that pressure causes you to run around and work really hard to meet the deadline you created. If you get all the work done (get done what you said you *needed* to get done), you feel the stress and pressure drain away, and you tell yourself, "Man, that feels good." But again, think about it; you are at neutral emotionally then think *"I need to…"* which created all that stress and pressure. You then do all the things you said you *needed* to do, and once you are done, the stress and pressure *you created* goes away—neutral to stress then back to neutral. And somehow, you think this is a good way to live?

This type of thinking is worldly thinking. Thinking this way creates stress—life stress or, as psychologists refer to it, psychosocial stress. You believe that you *should* have this kind of job. You tell yourself you *should* be earning this much money; you *should* buy this kind of house; you *should* buy that kind of truck. You think the car you have had for three years is no good anymore because you saw a newer, fancier car, so now you feel you *need* to upgrade and get the newer model with the newer bells and whistles. You tell yourself you *should* treat your wife better; you *need* to be a better parent; you *have to* take a vacation every year. You are chasing happiness in a manner (a way of thinking and perceiving) *that guarantees you will never experience happiness.*

When you think this way, when you view the world through a lens of *Should Statements,* the best you can hope for is moments of relief. And all this time, you are misinterpreting all of this as happiness.

And when you turn forty-five or fifty, you end up in my office, talking about the rat race you are stuck in: "I go to work, earn all this money, then turn around and hand it to all these guys with the bills, and I just sit there in my living room, watching TV. What is it all for? What is the purpose of it all?"

I used to work with a financial advisory company that has about fifty thousand employees nationwide. I was part of a luxury health care benefit. If the financial advisers wanted to access their mental health benefit, they simply called the company I worked for and spoke to me or one of our other psychologists. We triaged them and found the best match for their situation and symptoms. We also talked with them, helped them in that moment. I would hear the same story every day: "Dr. Parker, I came over from a company where I was only making $40,000 a year. They promised me $50,000 the first year, but I am on a $30,000 salary, and I *have to* go on commission my second year. But I *need* $55,000 a year just to pay my bills and not be so stressed, and I don't know how I am going to do it next year when the salary goes away, and I *have to* rely strictly on commission. I *need* to make $60,000 per year, then I wouldn't be so stressed." Then the next year, I would hear from the same broker again: "Dr. Parker, I've been working really hard. I got off the salary. I am doing okay on commission, but I am only pulling in $75,000. But I've got this bill, and that bill I *gotta* pay, and the kids *had to* get braces. I *need to* get up to $85,000, then I can feel happy about my situation." Then the third year, then the fourth year, the salary number they felt they *needed* to be happy and not be stressed always grew. I literally had phone calls from people complaining and feeling stressed out, depressed, and their marriages were falling apart because they only made $160,000 a year, and they *needed* to make just a little bit more, then they would be happy and not stressed. These are the people you envy. These are the people driving the big cars, eating at the nice restaurants, sporting the slick haircuts, and wearing $1,000 suits. And you think to yourself, *It's not fair. That should be me. Why can't my life be like that?"*

You are chasing a worldly dream that you think will bring you peace and joy, but the truth is, you will never achieve a sense of peace and joy because you are distorting reality when you view your life or the situation through a *Should Statement*, and this filter is not designed to create happiness.

Problem #2

The second problem with violating Fundamental #2 and viewing everything through a mental filter of Should Statements is, you give away control of yourself. Fundamental #1 says you can't control past, future, what other people do, think, or feel. The truth is, you (and only you) can control what you think, do, and feel in this moment, but you are choosing to *think* in a manner that gives control to the world, gives control to the past, gives control to the future. If the past is controlling you, if other people are controlling you, who decides what is right and wrong? Is it you? No. How many times have you heard this conversation from someone: "I don't know what I *should* do. I talked to Mary, and she said I *should* do this, and I don't know if I *should* do that. So I talked to Martha, and she said I *should* do this. But then I talked to John who said I *should* do something else. And then I went and talked to my pastor, and he said I *should* do something entirely different." Then they walk into my office and tell me all the different people they have spoken to who have told them what they *should* do and declare to me, "I don't know if they are right. What do you think I *should* do?" What is missing in all of this? Notice, the person asking the question is not considering *their own thoughts*, and they certainly are not considering God's will.

Now imagine I am standing there with an armload of boxes. I am thinking, *I've gotta get out of that door, but I can't open it by myself.* I see you there, and I begin thinking, *They are just sitting there. They should see I can't do this on my own. They should be courteous. They should help me out.* I begin walking toward the door, while you continue to sit there. When I get to the door and you have not moved, how will I feel? Angry? Mad? I might say to you, "Fine! Just sit there! I'll get the door myself!"

Now think about it; you open the door—I'm okay. You don't open the door—I'm upset. Notice your decisions are causing my emotional experience. But Fundamental #1 says that is impossible. So how did you get control over me? I gave it to you. Some people answer, "You allowed me to control you." Not true. Allowing means I offer something to you, but for you to actually have it, you have to receive it. You have to participate. If I allow you to have one of Judy's world-famous cookies, I will hold the plate up to you, but you have to reach over and take the cookie to receive it. No. I *give* you control over me. When we give someone something, they do not have to participate at all. If I wanted to give you a gift, I could mail it to you. That would require no participation on your part. Think about Christmas when we give gifts to people. We don't "allow" them to have something from the store; we go and get it and *give* it to them. Companies give raises. We give compliments to others. We would never say, "Hey, I am going to allow you to have a compliment from me."

It is the same with control. We freely give control to other people, whether they know it or not, when we put on the sunglasses of *Should Statements.* The moment I begin thinking that you *should* do something, my radar is on you. I am watching you. I am looking at your eyes. I am checking your movement. Are you noticing? Are you thinking? Are you getting up? Are you moving that direction? I am studying you because I have given you control and responsibility for my emotions. When I get to the door and you don't open it, I become angry.

And I will tell the world how crazy I am. Someone asks, "What are you so angry about?" And I say, "They wouldn't open the door! It is all their fault!" Are you getting it? Do you not do this all day long every day—blame the traffic, the weather, your spouse, the past? "I wouldn't be like this if that didn't happen to me." You are giving away control. And because you have given away control to someone or something outside of yourself, you then look outside yourself to satisfy what's inside yourself, and it cannot happen. It is impossible.

Problem #3

The third problem with Should Statements is that they create resentment. Consider this, the moment you don't open that door for me, it moves into the past. One second ago, you didn't open the door for me. Since I do my thinking in the present, when I think, *You should've opened the door*, then in the present, I experience the frustration of you not opening that door one second ago. In the past, two seconds ago, you didn't open the door. Since I do my thinking in the present, when I think, *You should've opened the door*, then in the present, I experience the frustration of you not opening that door two seconds ago. Two minutes ago, you did not open the door for me. Since I do my thinking in the present, when I think, *You should've opened the door*, then in the present, I experience the frustration of you not opening that door two minutes ago. Three minutes, three hours, three days, three years—the length of time is irrelevant. Since I do my *thinking in the present*, when I think, *You should've opened the door*, then in the present, I experience the frustration of you not opening that door, no matter how long ago it was. I am not carrying around resentments. No, I am actively creating them brand-new for myself every single time I think someone *should* have. I build resentments brand-new every time.

And we beat ourselves up. We point this filter at ourselves: I think in the present, *Lance, you really shouldn't have gotten yourself kicked out of college. I can't believe I screwed up so bad. What was I thinking? I should have focused more and stayed. Man, I'm so stupid.* When was that?—thirty-four years ago! But this is what happens. Think about your experiences as blips on a time line. When you don't do what you are *supposed* to do, it creates a negative emotional experience that is registered now forever on that time line. But when you do what you are *supposed* to do, it does not create any emotional experience, so nothing is registered on the time line. Every single time you don't do what you are *supposed* to do or do something you *shouldn't,* a negative experience is registered. So in the present, when you look at your past, you will only be able to see all the negative experiences every time you failed to do what you are *supposed* to do. And because in the present I am thinking I *shouldn't* have said that and I *shouldn't* have done that and I *should've* done this, then in the present, I experience *all those failures in this very moment.* Guilt, shame, regret, self-loathing all at once—all those negative emotions at one time cause depression to set in. And that depression feels justified because I look at my track record and see all the evidence of my failure.

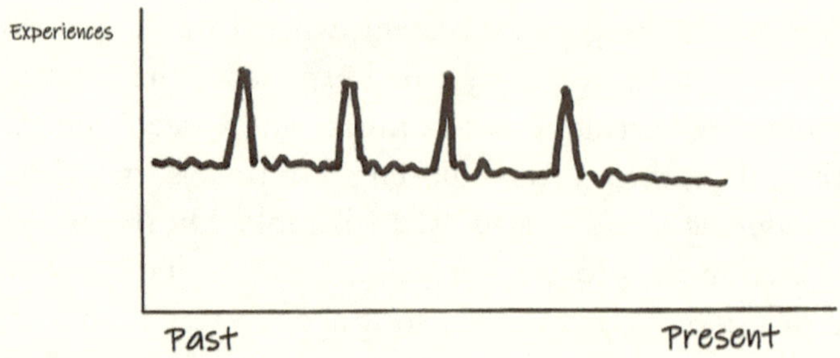

Solution

So what do you do? First, let me summarize what we have covered so far:

- You control how you think. How you think creates your experience, your feelings.
- Perceptions are thoughts. They are mental filters that we can choose to view our world through in the same way we choose sunglasses.
- A cognitive distortion is a particular perception that causes us to have a distorted view of the world, and thus, we create our own problematic experiences and emotions.
- One very powerful cognitive distortion is called *Should Statements*.
- By listening to the words we say or think, we can hear clues to when we are choosing to perceive our world through a distorted mental filter. In this case, Words like *should, must, have to, need to, gotta, supposed to, expect* indicate we have chosen to view our world through the distorted mental filter—*Should Statements*.
- *Should Statements* cause you to:
  - only have negative experiences (frustration and anger if you are viewing others through the filter; guilt, shame, pressure, stress, depression if you are viewing yourself through the filter).

o   Give away control of yourself to others the past and the future.

o   Build resentments toward others and create immense stress, pressure, guilt, and depression for yourself.

So what is the solution? At this point, you may be thinking, *I shouldn't say should.* If you thought that, reread that sentence again. "I shouldn't say should." You are saying *should* as you tell yourself not to say *should!*

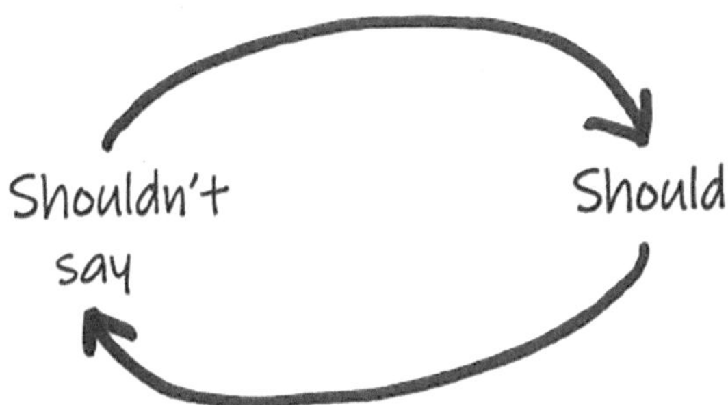

But that won't work. Notice that is like the snake eating its own tail. "I shouldn't say should. Oh darn! I said, 'shouldn't' and that is the same as a 'should,' and I am not supposed to say Should Statements!"

Instead, do this: Since you are the only one who can control how you think, take control! Decide for yourself if the *should* mental filter is good for you in a particular situation. Are you enjoying your experiences? Do you feel you are growing closer to God? Do you feel like a good parent? Good spouse? If not, then begin transforming by choosing to think differently.

Here is a tool I recommend you use to determine if a *should* filter is a good choice for you or not. Whenever you hear yourself think or say *should, must, have to, need to, gotta, supposed to, expect,* ask yourself this question: "Is it a law?" Whatever you just said *should* about, is it a law? Can you have them arrested? *Should* they be thrown in jail? *Should* they be fired? Is this a legitimate reason to discipline your child? Is this a valid reason to file for divorce or end a friendship? Is it a *law?*

If the answer is "yes," keep it. It is a good *should.* For example, "people *should* drive on their side of the road." Is that a law? Yes. So this is a good way for you to perceive this situation. Now if you believe that other drivers *should* drive on their side of the road, and you have determined it is a law, how will you respond if another driver is not obeying the law? Do you have a right to chase them down, get in front of them, slam on your brakes, and teach them a lesson? Of course not. So recognize this: for every *should* you put on others, you are putting a *should* on yourself. If they *should* drive on their side of the road, and they are not, then how *should* you respond? If someone is breaking a law, you don't have a right to scream at them. You *should* call 911. If there is a law, there is a legal remedy. If the fast-food guy doesn't serve you the cheeseburger you ordered and paid for but instead gives you a fish sandwich, do you have the right to slap him around, scream, humiliate him, cause drama? No. You know better. That would be silly. So if he *should* give you the food you ordered (contract law) but doesn't, then you are *supposed to* show him your receipt, try to work it out with him, or call for the manager. If there is a law, there is a legal remedy that you *should* respond with.

Now extend this to your life. If your spouse does something he or she *shouldn't,* do you have a right to scream at them? If your child does something they *shouldn't,* do you now have the right to scream at them, slap them around, humiliate them? No. But there are things you *should* do, steps you *should* take to save the marriage or responsibly parent your child. Invest your energy into doing those things instead.

Now, what if the answer to the question "is it a law" is "no"? Let's return to our earlier example. Imagine you have an armload of boxes you need to carry out to your truck, but you can't open the door with your arms full. You stand there, look at me, and think, *He should open the door for me! He should be courteous!* Now is that *really* a law? Can you have me arrested for just sitting there? Imagine that 911 call! "Yes, police department? I have a guy here refusing to open the door for me. That's right! Send the whole SWAT team!" That would be ridiculous!

If it is *not* a law, then choosing to view the situation through the *Should Statement* filter is not good for *you*! So what do you do? Change how you think! Transform by the renewing of your mind. Choose a different mental filter. Take off the *should* sunglasses and pick up a different pair. Change your perspective from *Should Statements* to *Preferences!*

Is it a law? "No." Then it is not a *should*. What is it then? It is a personal *preference*. It is what you *want*. Reapproach the situation with this new perspective and say to yourself (think) something like this instead: "*I would like* him to open the door. *I would appreciate* it if he opened the door. It *would be nice* if he opened the door. *I could use some help* right now, and *I would love it* if he helped me out and opened the door for me." Change your thinking, change your options, and change your experience.

Notice, when you think differently, you use different words. The computer program your brain uses to think is called the English language. So what you say is what you think, and what you think is what you say. By stopping and challenging the current thought process, you have to choose different words to engage the new thought process.

Now that you are thinking this new way (looking at the situation through a different filter, different sunglasses), reimagine the scenario: "You know, it would be great if he helped me out and got the door for me." As you begin walking toward the door and see me sitting there, what might you do? *Ask*! How easy did that behavior come to mind? Notice, how you think brings to mind options of *what to do*. Remember, it is cognitive behavioral. How you think will bring to mind a list of options for how to *behave*. When you think, *I would like…* notice how the option of asking rises to the top of this list for you to choose from. But imagine for a second that you are still thinking, *He should help out and open the door. From* that *perspective*, does the idea of asking for help rise up? How many times have you heard someone say this: "I *shouldn't* have to ask! They *should* know!" When you view the situation through a *should*, you don't feel like asking; you feel like yelling or demanding. How you think creates your experience *and* brings to mind different options for how to behave.

So back to the scenario. You have a bunch of boxes and are thinking, *I would like some help*, so you ask me, "Hey, would you get the door?" Now imagine I reply in an ugly tone, "No!" Notice what you just thought and felt? Maybe you thought, *Okay. Whatever.* Notice your emotional experience was mild, maybe disappointment but not anger.

If you are really imagining this scenario, then you probably see yourself standing there, leaning toward me as you ask for help. When I say, "No!" You see yourself say, "Whatever" and lean away. Notice, you move away from me. Why move away?

Because I don't control you! You can't read my mind. You don't know what I am thinking and, at this point, probably don't care to know. "Whatever." Your emotional experience is one of disappointment. You sigh and think, Wow. *I guess I will open the door myself* (which is what you would have done anyway if I were not there).

Now imagine if you were thinking I *should* open the door and that you *shouldn't* have to ask. You might think to yourself, *Oh man, he is just going to sit there like that? This is so frustrating. He should see I need help. He should get up. I shouldn't have to ask! But I will suck it up and ask anyway.* You then turn to me and say (probably with a forced smile), "Hey, would you get the door?" Now imagine if I said "no." You would instantly start getting angry. You would lean *toward* me and say, "What did you just say!" Notice, in this scenario, you don't lean away. Instead, you lean toward me. Why? Because you just gave me total control over you. You become handcuffed to me. Now more behaviors start coming to mind: demand, intimidate, yell, maybe even threaten. "Get the door!" I reply again, "No." You draw closer to me and grit your teeth as your eyes bug out, and you demand, "Get. The. Door!" You become angrier and angrier and begin demanding and arguing with me why I *should* get up and open the door.

If you think about it honestly, you will realize that you think and act and feel this way many times a day. Further imagine, you finally give up trying to make me get the door. How might you act at that point: stomp to the door, throw your boxes down, throw the door open, pick up your boxes and stomp out to your truck, drive angrily? And when you get where you are going, imagine how that conversation may go. You would probably vent to someone and say, "Man, you're not going to believe this! I had all these boxes to carry, and this guy refused to open the door for me!" Now notice, something in your past has total control over you in the present.

Who is creating all of these experiences, choosing all these behaviors? You are. And it starts with the instant you think, *He should…* After that, you lose. Once your reality passes through the mental filter of *Should Statements,* you have no choice but to feel something negative or nothing at all. Confrontational and dramatic behaviors will come to mind. You will have given total control of yourself over to someone else or the past.

Now walk through the scenario from a *Preference* perspective. Think, *I would like their help with the door.* Now you ask me to open the door, and I say "no." You respond by turning away from me physically *and mentally.* "Whatever." Feeling disappointed I won't help you, you instantly shift your attention from option A, I help open the door, to option B, you open the door yourself. You set your boxes down, open the door, and go on with your life. You will have forgotten me within five minutes and be focused on the next thing in your day that you *want.*

But if you ask me to open the door, and I say, "Sure!" You feel a surge of joy or appreciation. You get a moment of happiness. Where did that happiness come from? You! By changing how you think, you create the opportunity to experience positive emotions!

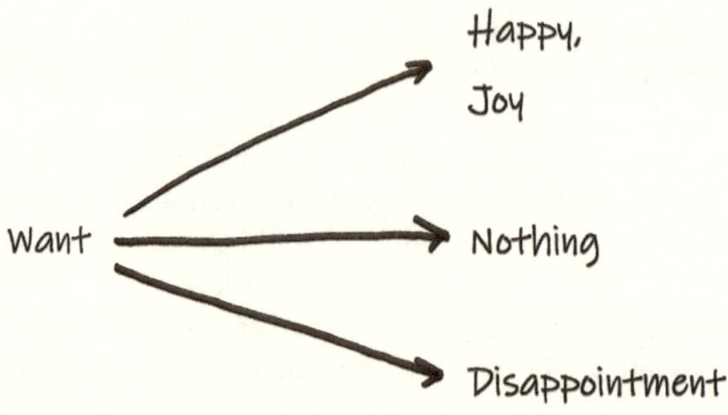

Now go back to the role play where I was a bundle of nerves because it was about to rain, and my car windows were down. Imagine if I said to you, "Hey, give me a second. It is about to rain, and I left my car windows down!" I run outside. But five minutes go by, and I have not returned. So you go over to the window and see me in the parking lot shouting at the rain clouds, "Go away! Go away!" You would think I am crazy. So now you understand that when people come into my office and they are upset because someone said this on Facebook or their spouse didn't do this or that, or twenty-two years ago, this happened, they are making themselves crazy by giving away control of themselves to other people or to the past.

I am *not* saying that other people can act however they want, and they don't have to face the responsibility for their actions. If someone has broken a law, prosecute them. If someone has offended you, bring it to their attention, try to work it out, or end the friendship. What I am saying is that no matter what occurs in the world, you can choose to experience it in a way that is best for you. Jesus said, "In this world, there will be trouble, but take heart! I have overcome this world." He tells us repeatedly, do not worry, do not be anxious, do not be afraid. He tells us these things because he knows we have an option to feel peace, joy, love!

In the Bible

You have just learned one cognitive-restructuring skill. This skill was developed by psychologists in practice and in universities. Through years of study and research, from Freud, to Jung, to Adler, to Beck, to Burns and so on, psychologists have continually researched the human condition and built on the discoveries of psychologists before them. Universities organize this knowledge and teach it to psychology graduate students so they may one day be able to help their clients. The average psychologist spends twelve years in college. After twelve years of formal education, they participate in an internship for one year then undergo at least one year of postdoc study or training. Finally, they become licensed. Keep that in mind as you read on.

From 1989 to 1998, I studied and trained to be a psychologist. I was licensed in 1999. By 2016, I had been a licensed, practicing psychologist for seventeen years. I know my craft well. I have used cognitive-behavioral techniques with clients in a variety of settings: jail, medical hospitals, mental hospitals, psychiatric prisons, and in my private practice. I created seminars on a variety of topics, such as stress and anger management, that were based on cognitive-behavioral principals. And as a Christian, I attended church regularly and read the Bible, some parts multiple times.

Then something happened in 2016 as I perused the Bible one evening. I came across the parable *At the Home of Martha and Mary* (Luke 10:38–42). Now I have read this parable before. And honestly, I never understood it. I sometimes wondered why it was even in the Bible. It didn't make any sense. And every time I read it, I wondered, "What the..." and just moved on. Honestly, I concluded that it was just stuck in. Have you ever seen photos of old scrolls? They are not beautiful rolls of parchment with gold lettering in pristine condition. No. They are tattered pieces and scraps resembling more that of an old puzzle that went through a house fire. I decided that this parable was on a scrap of scroll found in the bottom of a jar, and the archeologists just picked it and stuck it with another section where they thought it might fit.

But this day in 2016, as I began to read this parable in my Bible, angels entered my room and began to sing. A heavenly wind whipped up, and the letters of the Bible began to shimmer in gold and rise up off the pages! Actually, none of that is true. But it felt like that. Suddenly, *I understood the parable!* The parable begins:

> "As Jesus and his disciples were on their way, he came to a village where a woman named Martha opened her home to him. She had a sister called Mary who sat at the Lord's feet, listening to what he said. But Martha was distracted by all the preparations that *had to* be made."

At this point in the story, we have the setting. Jesus was out traveling and stopped by the home of Martha and Mary. Chances are, he did not call ahead given the lack of cell phones at the time. So what we have here is an unexpected guest. How do you feel about people just stopping by your house unexpectedly? Most of us really don't like that. And not just anybody but your boss! Can you imagine that? Ding-dong! "What the… Who could that be? Honey, are you expecting anyone! Oh no! It's my boss! What's he doing here? Quick! Pick up the living room! I will get a snack tray put together!" So in this parable, we have what is universally thought of as a stressful situation. Why do we think of these situations as stressful? Because guest *should* call ahead or schedule visits. They *shouldn't* just drop by! And we *should* receive guests with proper preparations: food, drink, clean house, etc. And what else is going on in this parable? Mary. She is not helping Martha with the preparations like she *needs to* be. No. She is in the living room, listening to Jesus when she *should* be helping Martha! So as you read on, recognize this parable is about stressful situations and other people not doing what they *should.*

> Martha came to Jesus and said, "Lord, don't you care that my sister has left me to do the work by myself? Tell her to help me!"

Now we have Martha's reaction to the stressful situation and Mary not doing what she *should*. Remember, Martha was too busy with all the preparations that *needed* to be made to pay attention to Jesus. She was distracted. And it is apparent in this last sentence that she is angry at Mary. Martha is complaining because Mary is not doing what *needs* to be done. And notice that in her anger, Martha feels entitled to tell Jesus what he *should* do! Have you ever complained to God that he was not handling things the way you thought he *should?*

Jesus's response to Martha is short and to the point. But his response is one of the most powerful, life-changing responses in the Bible. First, he says,

> "Martha, Martha, you are worried and upset about many things."

All the pastors I have had the privilege to listen to have said the same thing about the Bible. "It is God breathed. It is the truth." So notice what Jesus *did not* say: "Martha, Martha, there are going to be difficult and unexpected situations in life. You're just going to have to learn to deal with them." Nope. Jesus did not blame Martha's stress on the situation. And notice, he didn't blame Mary. "Martha, Martha, don't be so mad at Mary. I created some people to be a little special, and you are just going to have to be patient with others." Jesus did *not* blame the situation, and he did *not* blame Mary for Martha's stress. He told Martha straight up, "She is responsible for her stress." (Fundamental #1: We control what we think, do, and *feel.*) Martha is also responsible for not feeling connected to Jesus because she distracted herself by focusing on getting all the preparations done *she* thought *needed* to be done. Notice, she did not seek *his* will in this moment; she relied on *her own* understandings and *thought* processes. Not sure that is correct? Read what Jesus said next:

But few things are *needed*—or indeed only one.

Right there, Jesus is speaking to Martha about how she is *perceiving* matters. "Few things are *needed...*" Needed—sound familiar? (Fundamental #2: *Should, must, have to, need to, gotta, suppose to, expect.*) Jesus is telling Martha how she is *thinking* about all of this (what *needs to* be done) is what is generating her stress, not the situation and not Mary. Her best thinking and intentions are the very things that are distracting her from a relationship with Jesus. So what would Jesus recommend Martha do about this? Change how she thinks! Read on:

> "Mary has chosen what is *better*, and it will
> not be taken away from her."

Jesus is showing Martha that she is stressed, upset, and distracted because she *thinks* things *need* to be a certain way, and Mary *needs* to help her (and Jesus *needs* to correct Mary). Jesus stated that in fact, there is only one thing that is actually *needed*—all this, as opposed to Mary's *approach* to the situation (her perception, her thinking). He said Mary "chose what is better." He did not say Mary made the correct choice or that she chose what is right. Remember, *Should Statements* are designed to help you distinguish between what is right and wrong, not what is better. You *should* pay your taxes. There is no *better* way to pay taxes. When the concept of *better* comes to you, it is always a choice of things you *want.* Do you *want* ice cream or cake? *Would you like* to go fishing or to the movie? When you perceive matters through a mental filter of *Preferences*, you will choose what you *want* or what would be *better.*

So don't believe psychology, and don't believe me. Believe Jesus. In this world, you are guaranteed to encounter two things on a daily basis: situations and people. How will you approach them? How will you *choose* to think about your situations and the people you encounter? You have the choice between two mental filters—two sets of sunglasses. Which filter you use is entirely up to you. You can approach everything from the perspective of *shoulds, have tos, needs,* or you could begin perceiving the world through a lens of *Preferences* and

Wants. Remember, Jesus said that, actually, there is only one thing that is *needed.* In that case, everything else must be a *Preference.*

Still not convinced that you have been given the power to change how you think and that Jesus is encouraging you to think in terms of *Preferences* and *Wants?* Consider this: the Last Supper. Jesus realizes the time has come for him to make the ultimate sacrifice for humankind. He sits down to dinner with his disciples and tells them this is the last time they will be together. He sets in motion the plan for his death. He sends Judas off to alert the Romans to his location so the Romans can come and arrest him. He knows that, once he is arrested, he will be tried and put to death on a cross. According to many pastors I have discussed this with, from the time they finish with dinner until the time the Romans arrest Jesus, it is only a few hours. Two or three at the most.

Now consider something else. Imagine you go to the doctor's office one Friday, and he reads your MRI with you. Astonished, the doctor looks at the MRI and turns to you and says, "I don't know how to tell this to you, but you have a tumor in your brain the size of a softball. And where it is located, you should not even be alive. I am sorry, but there is nothing we can do. Unfortunately, death is imminent. You may only have a few hours. Maybe a couple of days to live."

What would you do? As you leave the doctor's office and head home, naturally, your thoughts turn to your children. What are you going to say to them? Knowing that this might be your last chance to talk to your kids and these words may be the last thing they hear from you, what would you say? "Get a haircut, and stay off that damned video game!" Of course not. You are going to think of the most important thing you want them to know. "Son, please listen to me. This is very important..." Knowing that you are about to die and will not get a chance to talk to your children ever again, your last words to them are going to be from the heart and what you believe to be the most important thing you can tell them.

So consider Jesus's last words to his disciples. He said one thing to them five times. Knowing he was about to die, Jesus repeatedly said one thing over and over. Might that be important? His last words? Do you know what Jesus said to his disciples five times before he was taken away by the Romans? Do you want to know? I will tell you, but then I want you to put this book down, pick up the Bible, and turn to the Gospel of John. Start at the Last Supper and read for yourself. Five times Jesus said, "Ask for what you *want* in my name, and it shall be yours." Notice, he did not tell them what they *should* do or how they *should* behave. He said, "Ask for what you *want*..."

Throughout the New Testament, we are encouraged and implored to begin thinking a new way. Paul told us to transform by the renewing of our mind. And repeatedly, we are encouraged to let go of the *law,* that list of *Should Statements*, and instead choose to love others and seek God's will. Begin challenging yourself to transform by shifting away from a perspective of *shoulds* to a perspective of *Preferences.* In all situations, simply ask yourself, "What would be *better?*"

Homework

I have always chosen to use the term "homework" because everyone understands the concept. Take what you have learned in class today and begin practicing it outside of class. But really, it is not homework in the sense that you do the exercises one time, fill in the blanks, and be done. I will not be grading your work; you will, every single day of your life.

Hopefully, you now have a clear understanding of the concept of restructuring cognitive distortions. Cognitive distortions are thought processes (mental filters) that we choose to view our world through much like sunglasses. And like sunglasses, it is the mental filter, the cognitive distortion, that causes our experience, not the situation or the other person. If we do not like the experience we are having or the options for how to behave that are coming to us, we can challenge the cognitive distortion and choose to use a different mental filter, different sunglasses, different perspective. In this case, we can choose to view our world through a lens of *Should Statements* or *Preferences*. These are two separate and distinct mental filters that bring us very different results. It is up to us to choose which one is best for us in any given situation.

So the "homework" I provide is a mental exercise. Each time you do it, you force yourself to identify and recognize your thoughts. Once you identify the *Should Statement*, write it down if you can and then decide if it is the best perspective for you. And if you think not, then you expend some mental energy reframing that thought (rewriting it) in terms of a *Preference*. By writing these thoughts on paper, you increase your mental processing of the exercise and thus increase your learning. The goal is to begin catching the *Should Statements* mentally as they occur and reframe them in that moment into a *Preference*. And as with anything, the more you practice, the better you will become, the faster you will begin to recognize *Should Statements* and restructure them into a *Preferences*.

Application

Beyond the obvious applications of improving stress, anxiety, depression, and relationships, shifting to a perspective of *Preferences* will vastly improve your relationship with God and understanding of the Bible. Throughout the New Testament, it is written over and over, "What do you want?" "Choose." "Which would be better?" But we look right past it and keep thinking, *Okay. What do I gotta do? What should I be doing? I want this great stuff they keep talking about. How do I need to be acting to get that?* We are a bunch of Marthas. Jesus and Paul keep inviting us, "Here's the party. Come on in!" And we reply, "How much?" They tell us, "It's free!" But we feel we *should* do something to deserve it. We continue to think in worldly terms—nothing is free. You *have to* pull your weight. We think in terms of *should* and *must* and *need to*. That is what we have been taught. We keep approaching Jesus like Martha. That is why we are distracted in His presence and can't realize He is here with us right now, waiting for us to simply ask Him for *what we want*. Once you begin to shift this perspective, you will be amazed to see your relationship with Jesus grow and the wealth of *good news* that has been right there for you this entire time in the Bible.

At least once a day, sit down with some paper and think back through your day. Try and count how many times you said or thought *should, must, have to, need to, gotta, suppose to, or expect.*

After taking an accounting of how much your thoughts were filled with *Should Statements*, select one and write it down.

For example, "My boss *should have* given me a raise today!"

Decide: Is that a law? Can they be thrown in jail? Fired? Is it a reason to file a lawsuit? Divorce them? Punish them?

If the answer is "no," then rewrite that sentence as a *Preference*. To truly do this, you will have to take a few moments and rethink the situation. What is it you *wanted?* What would you have *preferred? Appreciated?*

For example, "I was really *hoping* my boss recognized how hard I worked and just walked up and gave me a raise. I would really *like* to earn more money. Since I am *wanting* to earn more money, I could ask my boss for a raise. If he says no, that is his right. No law against it. But since I am *wanting* to earn more, I will begin searching for a new job that pays better than where I am at now."

Once you have written out the new thought (reframed your thinking, transformed your mind), say it out loud. Then take it to God in your prayers and *ask him for what you want.*

Also, notice how you feel after the *Should* Statement (anger, frustration, stress, guilt, depression). After you reframed the thought to a *Preference*, notice how you feel (calm, peaceful, resolved, disappointed).

Notice, as you change your thinking, you simultaneously are improving your mental life *and* your spiritual life.

Fundamental Number Three

A professor once told me, "If you're going to be a bear, be a grizzly." So here is a bold, declarative statement: Stress and anxiety are by far the largest spiritual, social, and medical problem facing the world. Boom. One study of a general family medical practice identified the top 14 complaints that patients presented with. Some of those reasons for visiting the doctor may sound familiar to you: upset stomach, diarrhea, headaches, backaches, lack of sleep, lack of energy, impotence, heart problems, etc. They researched the etiology (source) of the patient's medical complaints and made a stunning discovery: 76 percent of the medical complaints were caused by "psychosocial stress." This is a fancy term for "stress of living." Another 10 percent were caused by mental health problems, which is invariably anxiety and depression. So clearly, in addition to being a personal problem for people or a mental health issue for others, stress is clearly the cause of the bulk of our medical problems. As for spiritual, many pastors have pointed out that the Bible tells us "not to worry" or "do not fear" 365 times (one for each day?). Jesus spoke a great deal about worry, stress, and fear. So I stand by my statement: Stress and anxiety is by far the largest spiritual, social, and medical problem facing the world.

A lot of books, seminars, and sermons will spend the bulk of the time telling you about the problem and how bad it is. And more often than not, they never actually tell you the solution to the problem. I once sat down to watch a video of a nationally known preacher because the title was about anxiety. *Great!* I thought. *I wonder what [famous pastor] has to say about anxiety!* He went on and on for forty-five minutes, espousing the ills of worrying and being anxious. He cited numerous scriptures instructing us not to worry and not to be anxious. *But he never actually revealed any solutions!* He just kept saying, "Don't do it!" If that has been my experience, I am sure it has been yours. If you are reading this, you know the negative impact that worry and anxiety can have: You feel horrible; it interferes with your relationships; and it paralyzes your decision-making. You don't need someone else telling you how bad worry and anxiety are for you. You already know this. So out of respect to you, rather than making you read a bunch of stuff you already know, I will skip straight to the solution: *how not to worry!*

What if?

I label Fundamental #3 "*What if?*" There are a few cognitive distortions (mental filters, sunglasses) that are all similar in form, but the name gets changed depending on the subject you are viewing. However, they all are based on the same underlying thought process. So it makes sense to bring them all together under one category. You may have actually heard of some of these cognitive distortions: Worry, Assumptions, Mind Reading, Fortune-Telling, Jumping to Conclusions, Overgeneralizing, Personalizing, and Catastrophizing. When you think in one of these ways (sunglasses), you distort reality, which causes you to experience stress, anxiety, doubt, fear, hesitation, paralysis, helplessness, hopelessness, or sometimes even depression. You cause yourself to struggle in relationships because you can't trust anyone, and you may even experience paranoia. And all of these experiences make it difficult to believe the Bible, trust God's word, and hear the guidance of the Holy Spirit.

How it works

Anxiety is an activation of the autonomic nervous system based on a thought.

To fully understand that definition, let me explain how your brain processes reality: Imagine that you are walking through the woods. The sun is shining, and your skin feels warm. The air is clean and crisp. You could not be more relaxed. *Oh, what a beautiful day!*

you think to yourself. You look across the valley from your vantage point atop the hill with utter awe—a splendid view for sure. You think to yourself, *That's just a gorgeous view! I would love to build a house right here.* That reminds you of something: "House. Why are we going through so much toilet paper at home?" You make a mental note to ask your family about that later. But thinking about home now reminds you of something else. "Oh yeah, on my way home, I have to stop at the store and pick up toilet paper as well as sodas, coffee, dog treats and Funyuns."

Suddenly, a big ole bear steps out from behind a tree and roars! Now imagine everything that happens in the next split second. Instantly, your entire body tenses, your heart pounds, you scream and take off running the other direction. Emotionally and physically, you went from a relaxed state to an extreme state of tension in less than a second.

What I want to do here is slow that second down and open it up. I want to slow time down and show you what is actually happening neurologically (in your brain) from the moment the bear steps out from behind the tree until you turn to run. Having this understanding is really important for you to be able to understand anxiety and stress and how to shift mental filters so you don't have to experience anxiety and stress.

Back to the moment the bear stepped out from behind the tree. First of all, you are not seeing a bear. Don't believe me? Imagine it is nighttime, and you are reading this book while lying in bed. The lamp on the nightstand is turned on. Now imagine you turn the lamp off. What do you see? Nothing. So turn the lamp on. What do you see? The book? Nope. Let's try it again. Turn the lamp off, and what do you see? Nothing. Now turn the lamp on. What do you see? The book? Nope. It is not a trick question, but it is a very important technicality. You are seeing *light reflecting off an object.*

Back to that split second in the woods when the bear stepped out. This is grossly oversimplified, but I think it helps to have a basic understanding of how your brain processes information. The bear stepped out from behind the tree, and a beam of light from the sun traveled across the sky and reflected off the bear. It is now heading toward your eyeball. At this point in time, as far as your brain knows, nothing exists because the beam of light has not reached your eye. That beam of light continues to travel; and eventually, it strikes a nerve in the back of your eyeball. *Ding.* Once the light strikes that nerve, the nerve reacts by generating an electrical-chemical signal. That nerve transmits the signal to the next nerve, which transmits it to the next nerve and so on. Still, no bear. There is simply an electrical-chemical signal traveling down the optic nerve heading toward the thalamus. This region of your brain routes that signal (brain data) over to the occipital lobe. Once the data arrives there, the occipital lobe begins organizing the data into critical shapes, features, and textures. Still no bear. The data has just been organized. Now that the data is organized, it is moved to another region of the brain where it is processed and converted into a *mental image* ready to be identified. Think of it this way: Your brain takes the newly input data and compares it to information it has in a mental Rolodex. You brain thinks, *What might this be?* and begins flipping through the index cards, looking for a match: "Anteater? No, no. Aardvark? Nope. Hey, aren't those the same thing? Anyway, uh…beaver? Nope. Bear. Hey, we got a match!"

So the first thing your brain does is *decide* what the object is that you are seeing. Note, that is a *decision.* Have you ever been at a party, and you saw a friend of yours walk in? You looked across the crowded room and called out, "Hey, Steve!" The guy that walked in began turning toward you, and suddenly you *realized*, it's not Steve. Think about what happened: light, data processing, *decision*: "Steve." Then he turned and more light was sent your way—new light, new data processing, new *decision*: "not Steve."

It is extremely important to recognize that you are actively involved in deciding what your reality is. A bear is not inserted into your brain for you to process. In a split second, you are actively engaged in gathering data, processing it, organizing it, *deciding* what it all means, and then creating a *mental image* based on that data.

Now that you have processed the data and *decided* it is a bear, what's next? Well, how do you feel about bears? Now that your brain has identified it as a bear, that data is moved to another region of the brain where your brain does additional processing. "Let's see. Bears are large carnivorous creatures roaming North America and have been known to eat people. Hmm. That is a bear. I am a people. The bear is only ten-feet away. My car is three-miles back. I am alone in the woods with no weapons. I am going to say that this bear poses a significant threat to my life."

That is the second *decision* your brain made in less than a split second. And yes, it is a *decision*. Consider if you were to see the exact same bear at the zoo. Your brain would process all the data just the same. But since the bear is inside a government-approved enclosure, your brain *decides* the bear does not pose a threat to you.

So again, it is critical to understand your environment is not causing you to feel anything. In less than a spit second, your brain processes visual data, creates a *mental image*, and *decides* what the reality is (bear) and then quickly evaluates that reality along with the environment and other factors to reach a conclusion (*decision*) about the reality (threat or no threat).

Once you *decide* that the bear is a threat, your brain then sends a signal from the frontal lobe down to the autonomic nervous system. There are three major regions to your brain. The central nervous system is in your skull and what we traditionally think of as the brain. But there is also the peripheral nervous system, which consists of the nerves running throughout your body responsible for relaying information between your central nervous system and the body regarding pain, touch, and muscle activity. Finally, there is the autonomic nervous system. This section of your brain is comprised of the brain stem and spinal cord.

The term "autonomic" in Greek means, basically, self-govern or self-regulate. This portion of your brain operates without your direct conscious control. Your brain stem and spinal cord are regulating everything that is happening in your body 24-7: heart rate, respiration, perspiration, cell metabolism, body temperature, etc. You don't have the ability to exert direct control over this part of your brain. Try a quick experiment. Consciously choose to move your body temperature up to 105 degrees for three minutes then lower it back down. You can't. But if this region of your brain decided it was necessary for your survival, it would do exactly that, and you could not stop it.

Back to the woods. The moment you *decide* that the bear is a threat to you, a signal is sent to the autonomic nervous system that basically says, "Prepare the body to deal with the threat." In response, the autonomic nervous system causes the following to occur:

(Keep in mind, we are still inside that split second of time.)

- Muscles begin to tense up because you may need to spring like a cat and run really fast.
- Your eyes widen so you can draw in more light to get more data about the circumstances you are involved in.
- Your heart begins beating faster. It needs to now pump as much oxygenated blood out to your muscles so your muscles have the energy they need to save you.
- Your lungs are drawn up behind the rib cage to protect them from the bear, and then they are expanded as big as possible to be able to hold a maximum amount of oxygen. A deep breath is taken in to fill the lungs full of oxygen like a gas tank in a car. The oxygen is the fuel your heart will pump out to your muscles so they function properly and save you.
- Adrenaline is released into your bloodstream to give you an extra boost of energy.
- The liver dumps out a ton of sugar to give you more energy.
- Digestion shuts off. This is not a vital function at this moment. All energy is diverted to the muscles so they can save you.
- Sphincter muscles clamp up because, again, this is not a vital function at this moment.
- Sweating increases so that the body can be cooled off, like a radiator cools off your car. You are about to do something very physical.
- Your mental focus narrows and tightens down until you are only concentrating on three things: threat, fight, or flight.

All of the above occurs in less than a second: visual data received, processed, *mental image* created, object identified, threat determined, body prepared for maximum response, and mind focused on the threat and two possible immediate life-saving reactions.

And hopefully, this all makes sense. It is the fear response. You're walking through the woods, mind wide open, then the bear appears, and instantly, your body is tensed, energized, and you are mentally locked on the bear, ready to react.

Now, I tell you all of that to tell you this. Notice what exactly activated the autonomic nervous system. You considered the *mental image* your brain created from visual data, and then you *decided* it was a bear. Then you *decided* it was a threat. Notice, it was the *decision* the bear is a threat that activated the autonomic response, "*Not* the bear." So we don't actually need "the bear" to activate an autonomic response, we just need the *decision. Decisions* are *thoughts.*

Many thoughts activate the autonomic nervous system, but the autonomic response is the same in all circumstances. It is the nature of the *thought* activating the autonomic response that determines what we label the autonomic response. Here is what I mean:

- *Fear.* You are having an autonomic response to a threat that is *real* and standing right in front of you. The bear is present.
- *Stress.* You are having an autonomic response to a threat that is *real,* just not present in this moment. The bear is at the office; and when you get to work, you have to face it.
- *Anxiety.* You are having an autonomic response to a threat that is *not real* or is irrational. Your imagination creates a *mental image* of a bear.

Some examples to help distinguish between the categories of autonomic responses:

- As you drive down the highway, a car speeds past you and veers into your lane dangerously close to your front bumper. You feel *afraid* because you could have been killed. The threat is real and present.

- As you drive down a crowded highway, you worry that one of the other drivers may stop suddenly in front of you or try to squeeze in between you and the car ahead. You feel *stressed* because these threats are real possibilities, but no one is actually doing it at the moment.
- As you drive down a crowded highway, you anguish over whether to cook eggs tomorrow morning because they might have salmonella. You could be poisoned, have to go to the hospital, miss work, get fired, lose your house, become homeless, and lose custody of your kids. You are *anxious* because the threat(s) are not real possibilities, just figments of your *imagination*.

Prolonged stress and anxiety cause medical problems because, as you can see, you are running your body in overdrive all the time. If you drove your car 90 mph everywhere, always slamming on the brakes, then gunning the accelerator when you drove off each time, eventually, the car would begin to break down. And that is exactly what begins happening to the body.

And as discussed (and as you know), stress and anxiety are extremely uncomfortable and create a lot of mental health, personal, and financial problems as well as interfere with your ability to connect with God and hear his will for your life. So what do you do?

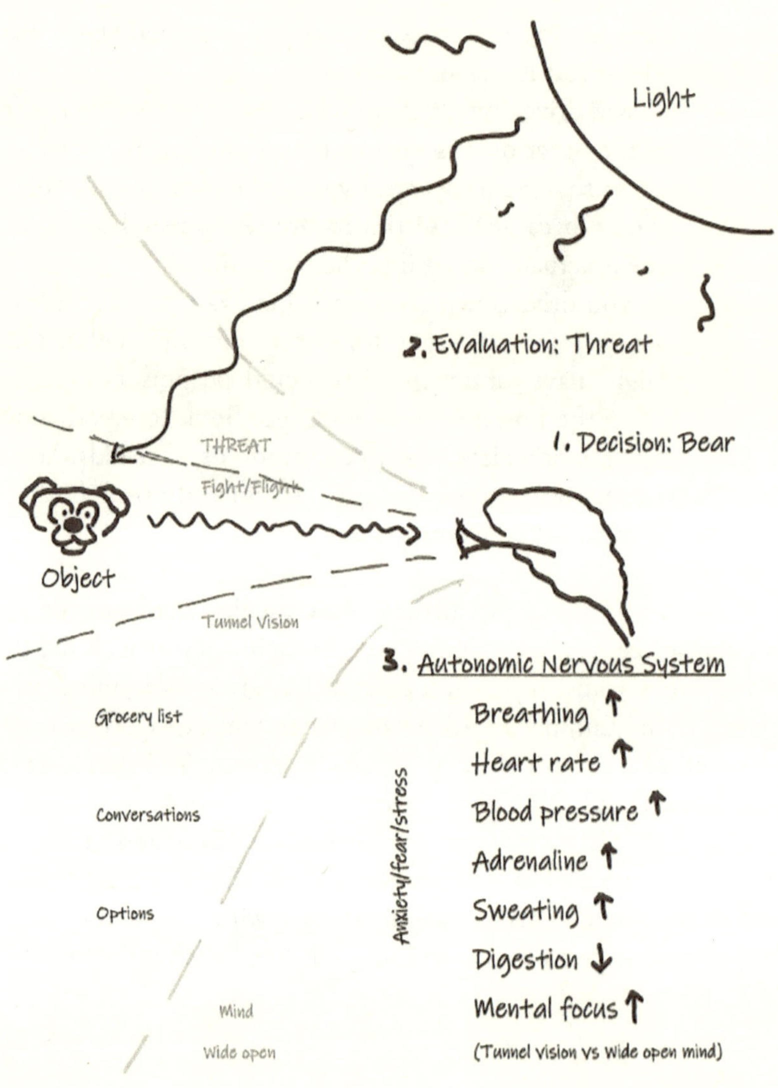

Solution

First, stop telling yourself, "Don't worry." That makes the problem worse. This is why I get so irritated with the books, devotionals, and videos that continually tell you, "Don't worry, don't be anxious." Trying not to stress causes the stress to grow. Let me show you how. Make sure you are holding this book out in front of you a little bit (not on your lap with your head bowed). Continue to concentrate on reading this page. Now take a moment to look just above the book at your environment. Maybe there is a ceiling light turned on across the room or a piece of wall art. Maybe just to the left of the book, you see a soda can. Whatever it is, concentrate on it for a moment. Keep the book in front of you, but shift your gaze to that other object. I will just use the ceiling light for this example. Check it out for a second, then bring your attention back to the book.

Now that you have resumed reading, try to do this: *Forget about the light. Don't pay it any mind. Forget it. Don't look at it. Don't even think about it. Look at these words but forget about the light. Concentrate on what I am telling you, and do not give in to the temptation to look up at the light.*

Okay, you may stop the exercise. You are free to look at the light now if you want. If you are like 100 percent of my clients and audiences, you suddenly found it very difficult to *not look* at the light when I told you *forget about the light.* When I do this exercise with people, I see them physically tense up as additional stress begins rising up in them. Their eyes narrow and lock in on me. They suddenly sit very still. Their jaw tightens, and they begin to hold their breath. Some actually break down under the added stress and have to close their eyes and look away. They often laugh and exclaim, "Gosh!"

Notice what is happening. Up to the point in the book where I told you to forget about the light, it meant nothing to you. But when I said forget about it, suddenly, it became an issue. Tension rose up in your body, and suddenly, you found it very difficult *not* to look. Here is the reason why: The light is in your peripheral vision, so it is *impossible* to *not see* it. As you try to do the impossible and *not see* the light, it feels like the light begins to glow brighter. As it seemingly gets brighter, you strain more to *not see* it. It feels almost like the light is calling out to you, "Look at me! Look at me!" You begin exerting more and more energy trying to *not do* something that is impossible to *not do.*

This is the exact thing that happens when you tell yourself *don't worry. Don't think about it. Just forget it.* The issue or worry that has you stressed out is a thought that *lives in your brain.* So it is *impossi-*

ble to *not think* about it. As you try to *forget* the issue that you find stressful, your stress actually begins growing. The more you try to *not think* about it, the more compelled you feel to think about it. The harder you push it away, the harder it seems like it is pushing back. So we actually increase our stress level when we try to *not be* stressed. We worry more when we tell ourselves *don't worry.*

Instead of telling yourself what *not to do*, tell yourself *what to do. Choose* how you *will think* about the issue. Remember, when you worry, you are using your imagination. The *mental image* you create out of your imagination is no different to your brain than the *mental image* you create based on visual data from your eye and ears. To your brain, those mental images are the same. So if you imagine a threat (worry), your brain will respond as if there is an actual threat standing in front of you. So change how you think about things. Recognize you have three optional ways you can think about the issue, whatever the issue is:

1. *Worry.* As discussed earlier, the only thing worry does is create stress, anxiety, physical illness, and interferes with our relationships, including our relationship with God. Think about this, *When you worry, you make yourself miserable today trying to avoid being miserable tomorrow.* Did you catch it? Read it again. When is today? Right now! It is always *right now, so it is always today!* Tomorrow is always tomorrow. Tomorrow never comes because you are continually in *today.* So if *you choose* to worry about issues, recognize you are choosing a lifetime of miserable *todays!*

2. *Plan.* When you choose to approach issues through *planning,* you plant yourself in the present and stay inside yourself (Fundamental #1). You recognize that the negative future event is *possible.* Others might laugh at you. You may struggle to pay your bills. You may not be offered the job. Your spouse might leave you. Since that negative *future* is possible, what can you do about it *now?* Notice, the negative event is not actually happening *right now.* You are imagining a negative *possible future.* So *right now,* the only thing you control in relation to that issue is to choose how

you are going *to think* about it. You can choose to come up with a plan *in case* it happens. What would be the best way to respond if others laughed at you? What would you do if you came up short and could not pay one of the utility bills? What would you do if they called you and said they filled the job opening with someone else? How would you respond if your spouse moved out? Remember, you can't control the future, but in the present, you can control how you think *about* the future. So you can choose to worry and create stress and anxiety or choose to begin making plans so you are prepared to deal with that *possible* negative future as best you can?

3.   *Dream.* Follow this logic. That negative future event that you are worried about has not actually happened yet. It is in the *future.* But you have determined it is a real *possibility.* Therefore, by definition of the word *possible*, that means that negative future event is only one potential outcome *out of many.* So take a moment and consider what other potential futures *are possible.* Some possible futures might actually be *positive.* Now decide. Of all the possible futures out there, which one *would you like* to see occur? Dare to dream. Set goals. Shoot for the stars! How do you want people to see you? How would you like your financial situation to be? What kind of relationship do you want to see you and your wife build together? Then ask, "What can I do to increase the likelihood my desired future occurs?" The energy that was anxiety and kept you awake at night now becomes the energy you use to build your dream. You are no longer anxious. You are excited, driven, determined.

Self-Fulfilling Prophecy

As a cognitive-behavioral psychologist, I work with people to help them recognize the power of their thought life. Whatever you envision, you will invariably create. If you think you won't get the job, you will be nervous and perform poorly in the interview and, thus, not get the job. If you think your spouse will be in a bad mood when you get home, you will walk in defensively and create tension in the home, and your spouse will respond to that tension negatively. If you think you will never understand the subject and fail the class, you will sap yourself of all motivation to try. And guess what, you won't understand the material, and you will fail the test. As my momma used to say, "Can't never could."

In the Bible

Funny thing is, God has been trying to teach us this very concept. In Proverbs, it is written, "Guard your heart for all the issues of life flow from it." Now the Bible is not referring to your physical heart but your "proverbial" heart. Your heart is your thinker, your feeler, and your chooser. It is your perspective of the world, your beliefs, your values and principals. It is your emotions. It is the way you approach your world, think about, and decide what to do next. Notice, the Bible is telling you that all of your issues come from *you* (Fundamental #1). And how *you think* is what is creating your issues, not other people, not the past, and not the future. Again, 365 times in the bible, we are instructed not to worry, do not be anxious, do not fear.

How do we *not worry*? How do we *not be anxious*? Read the Bible. The answer is written there. A friend just told me today that the number one underline scripture in the Bible is Philippians 4:6–7:

> "Do not be anxious about anything, but in everything, by prayer and petition, with thanksgiving, present your requests to God, and the peace of God, which transcends all understanding, will guard your hearts and your minds in Christ Jesus."

I have always been fascinated, though, how everyone who refers to this scripture only seems to remember the first four words: "do not be anxious." They will literally say to me, "The Bible says I'm *not supposed to* be anxious. But I don't know what to do!" My response? *Keep reading*!

"Do not be anxious about anything…"

"Anything." We are told no matter what is going on, whatever it is, there is a better way to *think* about the issue other than worry.

"…but in everything…"

The conjunction signals a transition to the reader: "You are about to be told the better way to approach *all* issues."

"…by prayer and petition…"

"By prayer" means you are to talk to God. "Petition" is a demand. We petition the government and *expect* the government will respond accordingly. So talk to God with the expectation that he will be faithful to you and keep his promises. In Isaiah 45:11, God said, "Command ye me."

"…with thanksgiving…"

Be thankful for all that he has done for you, and be thankful for what you are about to receive. In other words, *think about the positives* in life you have already experienced, are experiencing, and that will come in the future.

"…present your requests to God."

What is a request? It is literally something *you want*. Tell God what *you want*. And as we discussed earlier, in his last hours with his disciples before he was arrested, Jesus stressed to his disciples, "Ask my father for what you *want* in my name, and it shall be yours." So ask God for whatever you *want!*

"…and the peace of God, which transcends all understanding, will guard your hearts and your minds in Christ Jesus."

If you bring *everything* to God in this manner, *you will be at peace*, and not just any peace but a peace that *surpasses all understanding.* Have you ever known someone going through a really difficult time, but they seemed to be okay? They were calm? At ease? Maybe you said to them, "Man, I don't know how you do it. I would be going crazy right now!" Notice, they are experiencing a *peace that you cannot understand!*

Now, rewrite Philippians 4:6–7 in plain language that you can understand and identify with. Maybe it sounds something like this:

> "No matter what the problem is, take it to God, already knowing that God keeps his promises and will handle this matter for you. Thank him in advance for taking care of this problem for you, and tell him how you want it all to work out. Once you do that, you might be surprised at how calm and peaceful you feel to truly be in Christ Jesus."

Homework

Pulling all of this material together, I devised a six-step worksheet to help you walk from a place of worry through planning and over to dreaming (or envisioning). That worksheet is included in the homework section. Here are the instructions for how to use it:

1. *Write the worry down.* It usually begins with the words "*what if.*" If you are Jumping to Conclusions, you will skip past "*what if*" and just declare the negative future to be true. For example, you might worry, "*What if* I can't pay the bills?" Or you might skip worry and just jump to the conclusion, "I will never be able to pay these bills." In either case, write it down here in step 1.

2. *Now rewrite the sentence you just wrote, but this time, take out "what if" and insert these four words at the beginning of the sentence: "I am concerned that…"* So our sample sentence would now read, "I am concerned that I won't be able to pay these bills."

3. *Make a plan for that possible negative future.* Since the day may come that your bills are due and you do not have enough money, what would you do? How would you handle it?
   a) I will ask for an extension on the deadline.
   b) I will negotiate a lower payment plan.
   c) I will swallow my pride and ask my family to help me through this rough patch.
   d) I will sell my Xbox and use that money to pay my electric bill.
   e) ?
   f) ?

4. *What would you prefer to have happen in the future?* What is your dream? How would you like things to be? Write that down. For example, "I would like to be financially stable so that I can confidently pay all of my bills and have a little leftover to enjoy life."

5. *Make a new plan: What can I do to increases the likelihood my desired future occurs?* Begin setting goals and subgoals to achieve financial independence. Consider what you can do in the short term and long term of achieving financial independence.

    a) I will go to God in prayer, tell him what I want, and thank him for what I am about to receive.
    b) I will review all my expenses, eliminate unnecessary luxuries at this time, and develop a budget.
    c) I will cut up all credit cards and begin living within my means.
    d) I will start looking for opportunities to be promoted at work.
    e) I will look for new employment opportunities with better pay.
    f) I will consider getting additional training or education to increase my employment opportunities and income-earning potential.
    g) I will consider taking a part-time job to increase my income.
    h) ?
    i) ?
    j) ?

6. *Do it.* You are going to be amazed. When you work through the above five steps, something incredible will begin to happen. That excess energy (stress, anxiety) that was eating you alive gets converted into power. Once you start planning out how to achieve your future, that very same energy will transform from stress into hope, excitement, determination, drive, and motivation.

Application

On the next page is the Worry Worksheet. Do the following:

1. Make many copies of it. Set a stack of these worksheets on the kitchen table so they are readily available to you to use when you catch yourself worrying.

2. At least once a day, sit down at the kitchen table, get a pencil, select a worry, and work it through the worksheet. Don't worry if you don't have any big worries. In fact, it is best to practice with little worries. They are easier to handle. This helps you retrain your automatic thinking. Right now, when something happens, you automatically begin worrying and have to figure out ways to stop worrying. Each time you work through a worksheet, you make it more likely that when an issue arises, you begin to automatically respond by creating a plan and then thinking positively about how you would *prefer* the situation to work out.

Worry Worksheet

1. Write your "worry" down here: (e.g., *what if...?*)

   ____

   ____

   ____

2. Now rephrase the sentence, beginning with, "I am concerned that..."

   ____

   ____

   ____

3. What would I do *if* that actually happens or turns out to be true?
   a) ____
   b) ____
   c) ____

Now reframe the focus of the worrisome concern to a thought of a potential future that might be tolerable or even positive.

4. What would I like to see occur? (Dream!)

   ____

   ____

   ____

5. What can I do to increase the likelihood that my desired future occurs?
   a) ____
   b) ____
   c) ____
6. Do it.

Fundamental Number Four

Don't want—Do want

The fourth and final cognitive distortion to identify and correct I refer to as *"Don't want—Do want."* This title makes it simple, easy to remember, and easy to identify. It is also very descriptive of the shift in thinking you are targeting. This catchphrase refers to Negative thinking versus Positive thinking. How many times have you been told, "Don't think so negatively," or "you have to start thinking more positively!" Great advice. But again, they never tell you *how* to actually do it. And even though the Bible tells us to the benefit of positive thinking, we still default to negative thinking. Consider what Paul said:

> "Whatever is true, whatever is noble, whatever is right, whatever is pure, whatever is lovely, whatever is admirable—if anything is excellent or praiseworthy—think about such things." (Philippians 4:8)

What happens if you follow Paul's advice? What is the benefit of positive thinking?

> "And the God of peace will be near you." (Philippians 4:9)

If you want peace in your life, if you want to be closer to God, *think positively*. And remember Paul's circumstances when he offered this advice—he was in a dungeon awaiting death. So even in the darkest of times, what is the best way to approach matters? What is the best to draw close to God? *Think positively.*

But *how? Don't want—Do want.* First, catch yourself when you think negatively by listening for the word "not" or any variation, words like *not, don't, can't, won't, didn't.* When you hear these words, chances are, you are thinking negatively and may not even realize it.

Remember, when you think a thought, you are creating a *mental image.* The mental images that are generated in your mind based on data from your *image-a-nation* (imagination) are processed by your brain exactly the same way as the mental images you generate based on visual or auditory data (what you are seeing and hearing). So if you imagine something negative, you will have a negative experience (emotion) just as if what you imagined was *really* happening at that very moment. (See a bear—feel fear. Imagine a bear—feel anxious).

Don't believe me? How many times have you cringed because someone was talking about something gross? Notice, the actual event they are describing is not actually occurring at the moment. They are just telling you about it. As you hear the story, your mind recreates the scene through your *imagination.* You are cringing (negative experience) at something you are *imagining.* Your negative experience will feel so real that you will actually tell the other person, "Stop! That is so gross! I am going to throw up!" Your stomach churned, you felt nauseated, you made faces, and you might have even left the room. What you *imagined caused* your negative emotional experience and physical discomfort. That is the power of negative thinking.

So all day, you are killing yourself with a thousand papercuts by thinking negatively:

Negative Thought	Negative Experience
I don't want to get up.	You feel dread.
I don't like my job.	You feel disgust.
I don't want to deal with traffic.	You feel stress.
I don't have a choice.	You feel trapped, hopeless, helpless.

And that is just the first thirty seconds of your day! As your day unfolds, most people continue to think negatively. How many times has this been an issue or caused an argument? You said, "Hey, where would you like to eat?" They said, "I *don't* know. But I *don't want* fast food! Ick!" You replied, "Okay, how about Chilis?" They said, "Are you crazy? That is a chain! I *don't want* to eat at a stupid chain restaurant!" This conversation usually ends with an argument or leftovers from the fridge. Notice, they are disgusted and upset because they are *imagining* eating at restaurants they *don't want* to eat at.

A friend of mine was a waiter in college. When we talked about this cognitive distortion (don't want—do want), he thought back and realized, all the customers he ever waited on thought this way. He recalled that as a waiter, he would return to the table after giving the patrons a chance to look over the menu. He would smile and cheerfully ask, "Have you decided *what you would like?*" And every time, people responded in a very similar fashion, "Well, I *don't want* that, and I *don't want* that, and I definitely *don't need* that. I guess I *will have* this."

Notice how the customers had to first eliminate all the things on the menu they *did not* want or *did not* like just to settle on something that *doesn't* seem too bad? Why? And every time they declared what they *don't want*, they made a face of disgust, indicating that in that moment, they were having the same negative experience as if someone actually set that menu item on the table in front of them! Remember, they had not even ordered any food yet! So the disgust they were experiencing was solely from their thought process!

So shift from a negative thought process to a positive thought process by eliminating the word *not* from the sentence. This will force you to shift your thinking from negative to positive. For example:

Negative Thought Process	Positive Thought Process
Don't want	*Do want*
Can't	*Can*
Can't have	*Can have*
Can't do	*Can do*
Won't	*Will*
Won't do	*Will do*
Didn't do	*Did do*
Isn't	*Is*

Try this: Instead of saying what you *don't want,* say what you *do want.* Instead of saying what you *can't do,* say what you *can* do. It is harder than it sounds. Right now, the world has trained you to think negatively. Parents have told you your whole life what you *can't* do, what they *don't want* you to do. Television commercials show you what you *don't have* or *can't do* without. You are about to find out that negative thinking has been deeply ingrained in you. It is the thinking of the world that Paul warned us against when he said, "Do not be conformed to the *ways of this world…*" So you will probably find this exercise to be deceptively difficult. To say what you *do want,* sometimes you will have to stop and genuinely think—and think hard sometimes. Why *don't* you want that? What would you actually *want* instead?

Negative thinking
I don't want fast food.
I don't want to eat at a chain.
I don't want to dress up to eat.
I don't want to go anywhere expensive.
I don't want to eat too many calories.
I don't want to eat where there are a bunch of kids.
I don't want to eat where there are a bunch of drunks.

From this negative perspective, you are forcing yourself to *imagine* all those negative images and have *negative experiences* just trying to pick a restaurant. You are trying to prevent a negative experience but unwittingly creating a negative experience at the same time! I am sure you are making a frowny face right now just reading the list of negative thoughts (uncurl the lip). Often, when you get through all the thoughts above, you might decide to just stay home because *it is not* worth the trouble, only to think later, "we *don't* ever do anything."

Try the exercise right now: *Don't want—Do want.* If you *don't want* all those things in a dining experience, what would you enjoy? What would be nice? What would make it a good dinner? What *do you want?*

Positive thinking
I would appreciate eating somewhere that serves fresh-cooked food.
I would like it to be affordable.
I would enjoy something healthy because I am trying to lose weight and get in shape.
It would be nice to eat outdoors on a patio.

Now how do you feel? Crazy, isn't it? This is just a simple exercise, and you feel lighter and happier just reading positive thoughts about dining out! And some of you may have actually pictured a local restaurant you have been meaning to go try out!

Two other things to notice about shifting to a positive frame of mind: First, you now have search terms to find a restaurant on the internet! "Hey, Siri. Find a restaurant with healthy, affordable, fresh-cook options, and a patio." Siri will say, "Here is what I found." Do you *ever* try to search for a restaurant with the negative thoughts? Alexa, find me a restaurant that is *not* expensive, *doesn't* precook meals, *isn't* fattening, and where there are *no* kids or a bunch of drunks!" Secondly, and more important than creating good internet search terms, *you now have something to pray to God about.* No, not the restaurants but with everything else.

In the Bible

Paul wrote:

> "Do not be anxious about anything, but in everything, by prayer and petition, with thanksgiving, *present your requests to God.* And the peace of God, which transcends all understanding, will guard your hearts and your minds in Christ Jesus." (Philippians 4:6–7)

Yes, Paul starts off with a *don't.* And whenever I ask anyone, "What does the Bible say about being anxious?" They always hang their head and say, "It say's *don't* be anxious." *None* has ever been able to tell me the *rest of the scripture*. Because we are so programmed to think negatively, that is the only part of the scripture we hear or remember.

The rest of the scripture is where the *power* lies. Paul tells us, *don't be* anxious, but he quickly pivots and tells us what *to do* in *all* circumstances. (Everything is *all*). Paul tells us to pray a very specific way:

> *"…with thanksgiving…"*

Think about it. To express thanks, genuine thankfulness, you have to think about the *good things* in your life. What makes something good? It is, or was, something you *wanted*. So by starting your prayer with thanksgiving, you are priming your mind to shift from a negative mindset to a positive mindset.

> *"…present your requests to God…"*

"Present your *requests*." Requests. What is a request? It is something *you want*. When you request something, you have to think about how you would like things to be, how you would like the situation to turn out. You have to shift from *don't want* over to *do want*, from *negative thinking* to *positive thinking*. What happens if you actually follow Paul's advice? What is the payoff? What is the benefit of thinking positively? Read on:

> *"…and the peace of God which transcends all understanding, will guard your hearts and minds in Christ Jesus."*

You *don't want* to be anxious? You *do want* to be at peace? Get into a thankful frame of mind and tell God what you *do want*. In psychology, that is known as positive thinking.

Have you ever known someone going through a crisis? Wife left them? Car broke down? Company laid them off? But when you see them, they are smiling and relaxed? You may have said to them,

"Man, I don't understand how you do it! I'd be going crazy right now!" Notice, *they have a peace that is beyond your understanding.* That is the peace of God. You can be in the midst of the worst event you can imagine, but if you think positively, you will be at peace.

Homework

This homework is deceptively simple. Take some time each day to think back at the different times you said or thought something negative and how it felt and what you thought about doing.

"I *don't want* to get out of bed."

Write each of these down on a piece of paper and study them. As you read each sentence, shift your thought processes and begin stating something positive. Remember, this is as simple (and as hard) as removing the word "not" from the sentence. After you rewrite the sentence (shift your thinking from negative to positive), notice how you are feeling now and what behaviors are coming to mind.

"I *do want* to get out of bed." (Probably not a true statement, so keep going).
"I *do want* to keep my job."
"I *do want* to earn a paycheck."
"I *do want* to see my friends at work."
"I *do want* to go to bed earlier tonight so I will feel more rested tomorrow morning."

Application

Keep doing the written exercise every day until you find yourself doing it naturally as your day is unfolding. For example, I noticed a former client speaking to a group one day. He stepped forward on the stage as he said, "I *don't want* any of you to feel you can't let go of the guilt." He immediately stopped speaking, took a big step backward, stood silent for a second, then stepped forward again and corrected his negative thoughts by saying, "I want every single one of you to realize and believe you are forgiven so you may live in the peace Jesus provides us every single day." His mood changed from desperate to pleasant, and his words were received much, much better by the audience.

Additionally, ask your spouse, girlfriend, boyfriend, close friend, etc. to listen to your words as you speak. And if they ever hear you saying keywords (don't, can't, won't, etc.), they are to say out loud "not." In turn, you are to respond by rethinking the negative thought into a positive thought then state the new, positive thought out loud.

Fundamental Fusion

Trust me, I am aware that the brain, psychology, and the Bible are more complex than this book makes them seem. I wanted to boil everything down to a very simple level so that you might understand a few basic concepts and tools. If you can understand these simple concepts and begin using these simple tools, then you can successfully launch yourself into the more complex aspects of life: emotions, career, relationships with others, and your relationship with God.

Imagine yourself as a scrappy little sapling of a tree. How well you grow, how bushy your branches become, how green your leaves become are dependent upon the soil, nutrients, and everything you are tapping into. Right now, most of us are tapping into the world— the worldly way of thinking: "Might makes right," "do unto others as they do unto you," "get all you can," "money equals success," "don't let people walk on you," etc. So this is where you are drawing your nutrition from.

But we know, at an academic level, that this isn't right. We tell ourselves we *shouldn't* live this way. We *have to* go to church. We *have to* be better We *should* read the Bible. We *have to* get right with the Lord, etc., and so we see the church, the Bible, and other people living these beautiful lives, and they seem so happy. And we hear about how wonderful it is in Christ, and we know the Bible says for us to get in Christ, but we think that means we *have to* give up that worldly stuff.

So what a lot of us will do is pull our worldly self close to our spiritual self and try to live in both places. I had a friend a few years ago when Facebook was beginning to explode, and they were really excited about social media. They set up their Facebook page and posted many "cool" photos. Then a friend of theirs from church requested to be Facebook friends with them. What followed was six months of drama because they *didn't want* their church friends to see what they were doing with their other friends. So, on Sundays, they would snug up next to Christ, but they couldn't understand why nothing was really changing in their life. They traveled, went to Vegas, got crazy at party cove at the lake, but they still were not happy.

They did all the things they thought they were *supposed* to do: read their Bible, attended Bible studies. On Sundays, they sang to the music and felt moved, but when they walked out of church, they went back into the world and wondered why they still feel miserable.

For you to begin to experience the grace of God, you have to plant yourself in nutrient-rich soil and begin drawing it in. Once you begin drawing in this new way of thinking, which is all laid out for you in the New Testament, you will begin to experience grace and growth.

That is where the disconnect has always been. We approach reading the Bible as something we *should* be doing, which makes it a chore and makes us feel like a failure if we're not reading. Then when we do read it from a perspective of *shoulds* and *worries* and *negative thinking,* we get the wrong message. We read a parable and try to figure out what we *should* be doing and beat ourselves up for things we *shouldn't* be doing. But if you understand that the Bible is trying to show you a *new way to think,* then you begin to recognize that issues in the parable are not the issues. The issues that are presented in the parables are illustrations of how to *think* about things. Jesus is offering you a new way to *perceive* yourself and your relationship with God.

There is one parable I often hear people misinterpret. Jesus was approached by a rich man and who asked Jesus, "How do I get into heaven?" Jesus replied, "Follow all the laws and do everything the law says." To which the rich man said, "Heck, I do all of that." So Jesus then said, "Okay, then sell all your stuff and follow me." The rich man hung his head, walked off, and didn't do it. Jesus turned to his followers and told them, "It is hard for a rich man to get into heaven."

I have heard many people reference this scripture to say that everyone *must* follow the law, and it is *not good* to be rich. But that is a misinterpretation of this parable. First of all, Jesus *was alive* when he answered the question, so he had not yet gone to the cross and fulfilled the law, thus freeing us from the curse of the law. So at the time Jesus was speaking, the correct answer was, follow the law. After Jesus sacrificed himself on the cross, he created a new way to enter heaven—by *believing* in Jesus Christ. "Whosoever chooseth to *believe* shall not perish but have ever lasting life."

Secondly, by asking the rich man to give up his worldly possessions, he was asking him to choose: *trust in the world or trust in me?* Jesus did not say it is a sin to be rich; he said it is hard. It is just like my friend who couldn't merge their Facebook world with their church world. They didn't want to give up their worldly ways even though those ways do not bring true peace. So like the rich man, they are still searching for how to enter into heaven.

Fundamental #1 is about freedom, and whenever I have been talking to someone and they are angry and anxious about something, I will say, "What is Fundamental #1?" The response is usually, "Oh yeah, I can't control anybody else." But they are completely missing the point; it is not punishment! It's freedom! "I don't have the ability to control them, so they are not my responsibility! Yay! I can't control the past, so I can stop letting the past control me today! And my future is not yet written, so I can have any kind of future I *want* to have!" That is the beauty of Fundamental #1. You are free—right here, right now. You are in total control. When you begin to get that, it will excite you rather than depress you.

My son embodies this fusion of the Four Fundamentals. I have learned so much from him. My son has Down syndrome. Many people feel protective of those with special needs. They want to teach them things, help them learn. But the reality is, they have so much to teach *us.* The best example of how to operate inside all Four Fundamentals came from watching my son in a special Olympics bowling tournament. There were eight or nine kids with special needs assigned to two lanes that day. They were all are running around and happy. They hugged each other and patted each other on the back as they all arrived and placed their bowling balls on the ball return. None of them bothered to go sit down. Instead, they all huddled around the ball return, smiling and encouraging each other. They frequently checked the score screen above, carefully reading each name to see who was up next. When they identified the name of who was next, five or six of them would excitedly grab their friend, point to the screen, and urge him to grab his ball and bowl. "Oh! John! It's your turn! Oh! Ryan! It's your turn!" They would all clap and cheer for each other *every single time!*

And every single one of those kids bowled the exact same way that day. They picked up their ball, hurried to the bowling lane, and scrunched up their face as they concentrated intensely. They were careful to line up their feet in the correct position and then performed their best *imitation* of a bowler. They would take off toward the lane and swing the ball wildly. Bowling balls were often launched into the air, landing ten feet down the lane or make a beeline for the gutter. Occasionally, the ball would actually stay on the lane and slowly roll toward the pins. They would all stand at the line and watch the ball roll with great anticipation on their faces, some still striking the bowling pose. Even if it was a gutter ball, they continued to watch because you never know; it might come out of the gutter! You don't know! Once the ball finally made it all the way down the lane, it did not matter if it actually hit one or two pins or completely missed everything; all their buddies would shout, "Yay!" and clap loudly. Then the bowler would *run* back to the ball return, crouch with their hands on their knees, and stare into it the return chute, excitedly awaiting the return of their ball so they could go do it again.

As I watched, I realized, they were living in the *present moment (Fundamental #1).* The past was instantly gone. What just happened doesn't matter anymore. It was a *now* new chance to hit those pins. Instantly, they were able to let go of the past and focus on what is next. How long do you hang on to stuff? Further, there were no *expectations* (Fundamental #2) of themselves or each other, just a pure desire (*want*) to bowl with their friends. No one thought, *I should've done better*, or *I shouldn't have made a mistake*, or *he should've…* They just *wanted* to enjoy the moment. No one was *worried (Fundamental*

#3) about what others would think or that another kid might have nicer clothes or better hair or bowl better or what their final score might be. They only saw the *positive in every moment (Fundamental #4),* and that allowed them to celebrate the smallest of accomplishments. I began to realize, as I watched, that I was witnessing the Four Fundamentals in action, and I saw the power *we all have* to lead peaceful, rewarding lives if we could learn to *think* like they do, like *Jesus is trying to teach us to.*

Now compare that to us normal adults. I once had a chance to play softball with a superstar athlete. They had the equipment, clothes, skills, and the look. I was intimidated to be on the same team. But they shocked me in the first game. Every time they made the littlest of mistakes, they let everyone know about it. They threw their glove, fell on the ground, and rolled around even if the ball was still in play! You could hear them saying, "I *shoulda* got that!" "I *need to* concentrate more." "*What if* the bases were loaded when that happened?" "I *don't want* to screw everything up!" After a game, even if they played well, even if we won, they criticized their own performance to everyone and would sulk. *And I would think back to those special needs children and what a blast they had bowling.*

Right now, you are carrying something that you did or someone did to you. You are depressed or angry or anxious or ashamed or stressed or worried. But Fundamental #1 says you are free of that. So did Jesus. Fundamental #2 is *Shoulds vs. Wants.* This is a highly critical one because this is where we really start disconnecting ourselves from the Bible. *Shoulds: must, have to, need to, got to, supposed to—* these are key words that we hear ourselves say that cause us to put others or ourselves under a law, and then we judge others or ourselves harshly. We give away our control, and we build resentments and depression. We beat ourselves up. We evaluate ourselves as right or wrong. We judge other people harshly. This is the exact opposite of what Jesus is trying to teach us. You have one commandment; what is it? Jesus said, "This one commandment I give you: Love one another as I have loved you." How hard is that to remember? When you think about what you *should* do as a Christian, is that what comes to mind? Or do you mistakenly harken back to all the Old Testament commandments of "thou shalt nots?"

"Love others as I have loved you"—one simple instruction. How do we get to a place to operate from love and not judgment, letting go of the past and worries about the future? Why do you try to get that little speck out of your brother's eye when you have a log in yours? He is talking about how you approach the world, how you *think*. Martha and Mary: Martha got mad because Mary *should* have been helping in the kitchen and not goofing off in the living room. Her *shoulds* led her to be judgmental and so self-righteous; she thought she was entitled to tell Jesus what he *should* do about the situation. But think. What did Jesus say to Martha? "There are very few things in this world that are actually *needed*. Mary has chosen what is *better,* and that will not be taken from her." Martha is stressed and acting wrong because she is *thinking* wrong. Mary is at peace and chose what is *better* because she was *thinking* the way God *wants* us to think.

The second reason is once you think about what you *want*, you start to feel good. And once you get what you *want*, you feel good. When does that go away? Earlier in the book, I used an example about my car in the parking lot, windows down, rain starting, me being a big bundle of nerves, and you all told me to roll up my car window. You didn't tell me to stop the rain; we can't control the rain; thus we illustrate Fundamental #1. We can't control certain things. And when we understand that, it frees us to get our attention on the things we can control. Now, why did you tell me and why would I, in this silly example, to roll up my car window? I *don't want* the seats to get wet. Here is Fundamental #4: There are two ways to look at all circumstances—what you *don't want* or what you *do want*. You tell me to roll up my car windows so my car seats *don't* get wet. Here is what I do to myself if I do that. I am sitting here at neutral with no emotional state. I think, *Oh no, my car windows are down, and my seat is going to get wet. I don't want that.* Immediately, I see the car seats being ruined. I begin to feel intense pressure to avoid this future. So I run outside and roll up the car windows, so now my seats *won't get* wet. My emotions now move from stress and pressure back to neutral, a state of nothingness. I relieved myself of the pressure I put on myself.

Now, check out what happens emotionally if I think about the scenario differently and approach it from a perspective of *preferences.* What do I *want?* What would *be better?* I am sitting here in a neutral emotional state. I recognize it is about to rain. I begin to think, *I have had that car for sixteen years, and I like that it is paid for and reliable. I decide I want to protect my investment, and I prefer dry seats.* I might say, "Hey, give me a second. I am going to go out there and roll up my car window." Notice I start moving in a positive direction both emotionally and behaviorally. Because I am imagining myself taking care of my vehicle, which will keep it in good shape for another sixteen years, I am feeling purposeful as I head out the door. Then when I get my window rolled up and achieve what I set out to do, I feel accomplished. So by changing my *perspective,* I move myself from a neutral emotional state to a positive emotional state. When does this go away? It doesn't.

And we worry like crazy. What do they think? Why did they say that? What will happen tomorrow? Do I have a disease? We predict doom and gloom and begin to experience our predictions as if they are real. Research continually demonstrates that the majority of our medical problems are the result of stress. Either the stress wears us out physically and damages our body, or how we choose to cope with stress is killing us (alcohol, drugs, smoking, etc.). Rather than worry, we could make plans for potential negative events so we are prepared, then invest our energy into imagining positive outcomes and futures. We could dream. And isn't this what the Bible says? Do the birds worry? Why worry about tomorrow? Tomorrow will worry about itself. Rather than be anxious, pray, believe God will keep his promises, and tell Him what *you want.* Then a peace that surpasses all understanding will be upon you.

Earlier, I used an example of a waiter asking customers, "What would *you like* to order today?" Notice his question: *"What would you like?"* Notice the customers' answer: "Hmm. I *don't want* that, and I *don't want* that, and I definitely *don't want* that." Each time you envision what you don't want, you experience actually having it. I said to someone once, "Hey, I am making a sandwich. Do you want one?" And they said, "Yeah, but I *don't want* any mayonnaise." As they said it, they scrunched up their face and shivered. In that brief second, they experienced what it would be like for them to bite into a sandwich with mayonnaise. But the sandwich has not even been made yet! Where is this coming from? Who is creating a negative experience in this moment? We do this all day every day.

In this book, I have taken a lifetime of studying neuroscience, the brain and psychology, and boiled it all down to Four Fundamentals designed to help you with all challenges, including your relationship with God. Jesus boiled it all down even further: "What do you want?" And if you look closely at the Four Fundamentals, they all point back to that simple question: *What do you want?* Jesus emphasized this *new perspective* to his disciples in the garden of Gethsemane as he awaited the Romans coming and taking him to his death. I would suggest you approach *all the issues of life* by first asking yourself, "What do I truly *want*?" And if you don't know the answer, I bet, if you ask Jesus, he will help you figure it out.

I thought long and hard how best to close out this book and encourage you to continually practice reframing your thoughts and changing your perspective from negative to positive so you can begin feeling better and begin drawing closer to God. Then I realized, Paul said it best in Philippians, 4:8–9:

> "Finally, brethren, whatsoever things are true, whatsoever things are honest, whatsoever things are just, whatsoever things are pure, whatsoever things are lovely, whatsoever things are of good report; if there be any virtue, and if there be any praise, think on these things. Those things, which ye have both learned, and received, and heard, and seen in me, do: and the God of peace shall be with you."

The Four Fundamentals Summarized

Fundamental #1: Control

The truth is, you control very little in this world. You can't change the past or the future and you can't control other people. What you can actually control is *how you think, what you do and what you feel in the present moment.* Coming to accept and believe this fundamental truth—that you are fully responsible for your experiences and emotions frees you to now take control of your life and begin creating the experiences you would like and have longed for, as well as unshackle yourself from the past and from others. As Jesus quipped, "Why are you trying to get that speck of dust out of your brother's eye?"

Fundamental #2: Expectation

By thinking in terms of *Should (must, have to, need to, gotta, supposed to),* we create laws in our lives that we apply to ourselves and others as if they are governmental or spiritual statutes worthy of punishment. In doing so, we restrict our experiences to failure, frustration, anger, guilt, shame or nothing. The truth is, Jesus came to fulfill the law and gave you one commandment: love. Jesus said there are very few things in this world that are actually *needed.* When you choose to view your world through a lens of *preferences* (wants) and begin making choices based on *what would be better* (as Jesus suggested), you control your own experiences and destiny. You create the opportunity to feel success, joy, happiness and freedom—and that will not be taken from you.

Fundamental #3: Worry

The Bible tells us 365 time not to worry. But still we worry a tremendous amount about the future and what others think or might do. This is called Fortune Telling and Mind Reading. The truth is, we cannot predict the future or read other people's minds. When we engage in this distorted thinking, we create stress, anxiety, fear and anger for ourselves. We feel a false sense of control and begin to act in fear on what we imagine, not reality. We are trusting ourselves and not God. The truth is, we are intelligent creatures with the mental ability to identify possible concerns that might arise, and we have a helper to guide us. By shifting our perspective away *from worry to planning*, we increase our ability to control our lives and be prepared for problems. Now, if we make one additional cognitive shift and use our capacity to *dream (identify positive futures or interactions)*, we truly begin to take control of the direction our life is going and can start building positive relationships and better futures. Take your concerns and dreams to God in prayer and begin to experience a peace that surpasses all understanding.

Fundamental #4: Negative vs Positive Thinking

When we think negatively, we create negative images in our mind and, in the present moment, have a negative experience. We miss out on so many enjoyable, wonderful experiences because of this bias in our thinking. There are two sides to every coin. You choose which side you will focus on. Create negative experiences or *create positive experiences?* Focus on the problem or *focus on the solution?* By choosing to think about whatever is true, lovely, noble or worthy and doing what we already know to do, then we will be with the God of peace.

Testimonials

"This is revelational stuff."—Jeremy S.

"I have been in therapy for many years, but this is the first time I have been given an opportunity to have a genuine, authentic, real life."—Sean C.

"My family has had nothing but peace since we began applying the Four Fundamentals! We now live in the promise of God every day!"—Jofaya M.

"This is life changing! Quote me on that!"—Erin S.

"Now there are fewer Ping-Pong balls bouncing around in the mental dryer."—Chris M.

About the Author

Dr. Parker is a licensed psychologist in Wichita, Kansas. He enjoys riding motorcycles and spending time with his wonderful wife and the greatest son ever. Dr. Parker served in the United States Navy for eight years, began his study of psychology in 1989, earned a bachelor's in 1991, a master's in 1995, a doctorate in 1998, and was licensed in 1999. Dr. Parker served as the chief psychologist for a nationwide HMO for many years then, in 2005, entered private practice full-time. His work has taken him inside psychiatric prisons and hospitals, jails, and drug rehab centers. Up until 2019, the bulk of his practice centered around forensic psychology, particularly the highly emotional and contentious field of divorce and child custody. Dr. Parker is routinely sought out to speak at conferences regarding his expertise in forensic psychology. For years, in addition to his clinical work, Dr. Parker has conducted free seminars and classes designed to demystify psychology and make it useful to people in their everyday life, especially their spiritual lives. Dr. Parker is most well-known for helping people see how to use simple psychological reframing techniques to gain control over their mood and to begin developing a true relationship with God.

Dr. Parker routinely posts educational videos on his YouTube channel: *Crash Course Academy*, which can also be accessed from his free website, www.CrashCourseAcademy.net.

www.ingramcontent.com/pod-product-compliance
Lightning Source LLC
Chambersburg PA
CBHW022034150726
47990CB00002B/959